Belair Best Practice

Teaching Art 7–11

Published by Collins under the Belair imprint

Collins is an imprint of HarperCollins*Publishers*

77 – 85 Fulham Palace Road
Hammersmith
London W6 8JB

Browse the complete Collins catalogue at
www.collinseducation.com

10 9 8 7 6 5 4 3 2 1

ISBN-13 978 0 00 745562 1

Nigel Meager asserts his moral right to be identified
as the author of this work

British Library Cataloguing in Publication Data

A Catalogue record for this publication is available
from the British Library

Cover concept by Mount Deluxe
Cover design by Lodestone Publishing Limited
Internal design by SteersMcGillanEves
Photography by Nigel Meager
Edited by Alison Sage
Proofread by Gaby Frescura
Index by Eleanor Holme

Photographs:
p.34 *Surprised!* by Henri Rousseau, 1891, Bought, with the aid
of a substantial donation from the Hon. Walter H. Annenberg,
1972 © The National Gallery, London, NG6421;
p.46 *Landscape Sketch II* by Károly Markó (1793–1860),
this work is in the public domain;
p.61 *Head of Catherine Lampert 1986* © Frank Auerbach,
courtesy Marlborough Fine Art, private collection; *Head of
Julia* 1989 © Frank Auerbach, courtesy Marlborough Fine Art,
private collection
p.72 *Field (American)* by Antony Gormley, 1991, Terracotta.
Photograph by Joseph Coscia, JR, Courtesy of White Cube
p.84 ©Perig/Shutterstock.com ; © WH CHOW/Shutterstock.
com; ©Stephen Finn/Shutterstock.com;
p.85 ©Chris Green/Shutterstock.com; © Veniamin Kraskov/
Shutterstock.com
p.88 © Palabra/Shutterstock.com
p.102 and 103 photographs taken at The Robert and Lisa
Sainsbury Collection, The University of East Anglia by Nigel
Meager in 2012.
p.119 *The Mule Track* by Paul Nash, 1918, ©Imperial War
Museums (Art. IWM ART 1153)

Printed and bound by
Printing Express Limited, Hong Kong

Acknowledgements

The publication of the original edition of this book,
Teaching Art at Key Stage 2, in 1995, would not have
been possible without the support and collaboration of
teachers and children in a wide range of primary schools
from across Wales. Dr John Steers, the former General
Secretary of the National Society of Art and Design,
saw the potential of this work and offered unstinting
advice and support throughout the life of *Teaching Art
at Key Stage 2* from its first publication through three
reprints and up to the publication of this new edition.
I am grateful to Lesley Butterworth, the current General
Secretary of NSEAD, for the preface of this new edition.

Teaching Art at Key Stage 2 was co-authored by Julie
Ashfield. Julie also supported the work in Cardiff
undertaken for this book. Julie Ashfield has always
been a creative dynamo, willing to share ideas and open
to new directions. Her enthusiasm and knowledge are
an inspiration.

All those involved in the publication of *Teaching Art 7–11*
owe a big thank you to the teachers and children of
three primary schools. Llanedeyrn Primary School and
All Saints Church in Wales Primary School from Cardiff
and Dussindale Primary School in Norwich. All the
teachers at these schools were open-minded and
encouraging at every stage of this project. The majority
of the work was undertaken at Dussindale Primary
School. Thank-you to Jane Worsdale, head teacher,
and Sally Coulter, deputy head teacher, who made
this possible.

Particular thanks to Lee Newman, Alison Sage and
Aimée Walker from Harper Collins for all their support
and their work in editing and refining the text and
images. Thanks to Jon Ashford and Richard McGillan
of SteersMcGillanEves for the design.

Belair Best Practice
Teaching Art 7–11

By Nigel Meager

Contents

The origins of
Teaching Art 7–11

Teaching Art 7–11 is a new and re-worked edition of *Teaching Art at Key Stage 2*, originally published by the National Society for Education in Art and Design (NSEAD) in association with Visual Impact Publications. This was a sequel to *Teaching Art at Key Stage 1*, which had developed out of the Visual Impact Project in West Glamorgan, Wales – an innovative project which allowed artists to work in the classroom with primary school children. This partnership between artist and teacher led to a sharing of professional expertise and improved strategies for teaching art. The idea won support from the former West Glamorgan Education Authority and Arts Council Wales and The Calouste Gulbenkian Foundation, which went on to support the publication of *Teaching Art at Key Stage 1*.

Teaching Art 4–7 and *Teaching Art 7–11*

In many ways, *Teaching Art 7–11* follows a similar pattern to *Teaching Art 4–7*.

The activities described in *Teaching Art 4–7* build on one another. A typical sequence begins with a form of guided talking and is followed by ideas to help children experiment and explore the visual qualities. Children go on to learn or revise a process, technique or skill and then finish by making an art, craft or design object. Woven into the text are ideas about how teachers can encourage children to talk about actual examples of art and design.

However, there is one specific difference between the two books. In *Teaching Art 4–7*, each of the eight chapters has as its theme one of the visual qualities: Shape, Pattern, Colour, Form, Space, Tone, Texture and Line. In contrast, the chapters in *Teaching Art 7–11* are a series of project examples. The implication is that with older children, the formal strategies for developing the visual language of art (work with visual qualities such as colour, tone, texture, etc.) are more likely to be integrated into projects that progressively open up potential for both breadth and depth in the children's art and design. In many cases, the visual qualities themselves become subsumed into projects that might have as a focus a range of features such as language, imagination, ideas, skills and examples of adult art.

How to use *Teaching Art 7–11*

In *Teaching Art 7–11* the chapters are not intended to form a prescriptive system or scheme of work, rather they can be used to prompt ideas for units of work appropriate to individual schools. So, no attempt is made in this book to suggest a particular scheme of work that is to be progressively introduced. Teachers may want to plan an art programme rather like a maths scheme of work, but because the nature of art and design is so broad, and because the individual art experience of individual children and schools is so diverse, it is inappropriate here to write a scheme or programme that would work for each and every case. So the idea behind this book is to show as clearly as possible to teachers who are not necessarily art specialists, a set of examples of how art and design could be taught.

Teaching Art 4–7 advocated the value of teaching a foundation of basic skills and concepts. An implication for older children is that if they have been introduced to both the visual language of art and to a set of core skills and principles from the age of four, they will progress quickly towards more sophisticated art work. The importance of providing a foundation of work for four to seven year olds cannot be over emphasised. However, not all seven to eleven year olds will have this foundation of skills and concepts in place. For this reason, many of the activities appropriate for four to seven year olds are equally suitable for older children. It would therefore be possible to use the activities described in *Teaching Art 4–7* as starting points for the more advanced projects that will challenge older children. The activities in *Teaching Art 4–7* could then become warm up exercises and a way of revising basic concepts and skills for many of the projects in this book. In any case, there is a natural overlap between the two books as it is essential to place more advanced work in the context of what younger children have already learned. The overlap also allows teachers who have not read *Teaching Art 4–7* to implement the projects described here. So the relationship between the two volumes is a balance between the educational need for progressive continuity (including more advanced and progressive projects for seven to eleven year olds) and the recognition that these children may still be working at a more basic level, and may not have not been introduced to this way of thinking about art.

Teaching Art at Key Stage 2, was co-authored by Julie Ashfield, an art advisory teacher for Cardiff County Council in Wales. Julie became a key member of the Cardiff Arts Support Team (CAST) and has contributed many ideas and supported this current edition, working with the author in two Cardiff schools whose children feature in a number of the chapters – Llanedeyrn Primary School and All Saints Church in Wales Primary School.

Finally, all the projects described have been tried and tested in the classroom. The author has both taught and photographed the work as it progresses and these photographs carry a great deal of information. It is worthwhile looking carefully at these images for clues about how the children are working and how the classroom is set up. Above all, the photographs are designed to communicate something of the creative atmosphere of teaching and learning in this most enjoyable of subjects.

Lesley Butterworth, General Sectretary, NSEAD

Practical issues

All the projects are designed for whole class teaching. Occasionally it will be more practical to rotate groups of children to work on a skill where space is limited or tools and equipment need to be shared. Sometimes, the logistical nature of art and design activities in the confines of a classroom will mean that additional adult help will be welcome. Some of the projects took place at Dussindale Primary School where parents are regularly invited into the classroom. On a number of occasions I took advantage of this, and the whole class of around 30 children worked on a practical activity at the same time. Additional adult support can prevent children becoming disorganised because they have forgotten to follow the specific instructions about a technique. Extra adult can also offer logistical support organising materials, tools and equipment. However, throughout I have given advice about techniques with the aim of helping children to become self-sufficient and in control of their practical work. In this way, they can continue independently without direct adult intervention.

The general content of each chapter is described by the title. Each chapter is further broken down into sessions. These should give the reader an indication of how each block of teaching and learning has been planned. Inevitably, different schools will have different timetables and different ways of organising the curriculum, so for some schools a session may need two or more lessons to complete; in others, where occasionally a whole day might be allocated for a project, a teacher could plan several sessions to run together.

Each session is further divided into smaller blocks of work indicated by sub-headings. These sub-headings suggest the themes of the various activities and experiences which build together progressively to attain the anticipated outcome. You may find these sub-headings useful for more formal lesson planning, if this is required. There is also a materials and equipment check list on page 126, but each of the sessions is also concluded with a list of what you will need.

The broader practical message here is to consider using the text and photographs as an inspiration and guide to planning and teaching your own art and design lessons, rather than as a how-to-do-it recipe to be followed to the letter.

Principles in practice

To get the most out of *Teaching Art 7–11*, it is worth asking the question: what are the principles which underpin the planning and implementation of the projects described in this book? Thinking about these underlying principles will help you read between the lines of the text, which is quite detailed and specific, and adapt what you discover to plan work suited to your own situation. This is important because each class, school, and curriculum can be different in some degree.

So, you will have to fashion these projects so that they are appropriate for your own children, school, curriculum and broader culture where you work. These are the principles:

Talking

Talking is a lynchpin of much contemporary pedagogical practice. Primary school children talk in pairs, in small groups and with an adult. They take part in question and answer sessions and in discussions with the whole class. They listen to what others say. Talking helps children to form ideas. Talking helps build understanding. Moreover, what is said to children will guide what they do. This may seem a trite point, but in art and design it is sometimes thought that achieving success is a matter of innate talent, or that art is essentially mysterious and words only get in the way. It is just the reverse. Talking helps children focus. In particular, it slows down the process of seeing. Asking children to talk about what they can see, and recording this in a list or word bank will greatly improve their drawing.

I remember working with a Welsh educator and artist, David Petts, who insisted on the value of talk. On one memorable occasion, before asking children to draw what at first sight appeared to be rather mundane stones and rocks, he introduced children to the concept of 'touching with your eyes'. This meant using your eyes as if they were fingers, gradually and slowly moving across the surface of the stone, imagining that you could feel every crevice, indentation and detail simply by looking. He asked children to talk about what they had found. There was so much to say! Children talked for a surprising length of time about something as ordinary as a stone. The resulting drawings were magnificent. The rocks and stones became magical, each with a unique identity. Throughout *Teaching Art 7–11*, ideas for talking feature in different ways. Please don't skimp or rush through opportunities for talk. There will be a direct correlation between the quality of drawings and the quality of talk.

In this book, what the teacher is saying has deliberately been made a focal point of the design:

Find the middle of your paper. Look at the building. Find a shape near the middle of the building. Try starting the drawing by putting that first shape in the middle of the paper. Next, look for the shapes that are near the first one and then add those to your drawing. Your drawing will grow bit by bit as you add in more of the shapes you can see. Don't forget that most of the shapes will have other shapes inside them. Think carefully about where each new shape should go. Only draw the outline shape of the whole building after you have drawn most of the important window and door shapes.

Reading these examples of how a teacher can introduce a project will help to explain how this particular way of teaching art works. It is a fact that I almost never show children how to draw. I do, however, spend considerable time talking about how to go about drawing. This book demonstrates that *you don't need to be good at art to teach it well*. By paying attention to what you say to children and by valuing talk, you will help children make great progress with their art, whether you feel you are 'good' at art or not.

Exploring and experimenting

As you read how the various themes of each chapter unfold, you will notice how often children are asked to collect, experiment, investigate and explore. There are frequent references to starting points and warm-up activities. Sometimes these will be about exploring one of the visual qualities: shape, line, pattern, colour, form, space, tone, texture. On other occasions these preliminary activities focus on practising using materials, or on learning a particular technique. Allowing children to work in this more open and abstract way, without thinking about making a picture, for example, is liberating. For example, if children can practice mixing colours before making a painting, they will develop an understanding of just what they can achieve as they find out how to use brushes, get used to the properties of paint and discover the limitless potential of colour. This builds confidence. It is particularly valuable for children who do not see themselves as 'good at art'. It is always tempting to cut to the chase with art projects and teachers with limited time available may sometimes feel it is best to get on with making an end product right away. But this can be a mistake. Time spent allowing children to explore and experiment will be richly rewarded. The experiments themselves can look wonderful. There is just so much to look at and talk about.

Learning skills and techniques

To succeed in making art and design end products, children need to learn a variety of skills and techniques. In this book you will find examples of how to help children draw, paint, use clay, collage, construct, illustrate, print, and use a camera. Sometimes advice is set out in considerable detail. Use the index to find these various processes quickly in the text. There are, of course, many other possible approaches to these procedures. Whichever method you decide to introduce (for example, a particular way of painting), I find it best to break down the technique into the smallest component parts. Talking clearly about how each component part slots together to make a process and then offering children the chance to practice and learn from mistakes before they make a finished work is most valuable. A good example of this is the specific reminder to children about a particular painting technique (on page 48).

Using appropriate technology

Information and communication technology (ICT), is a vital part of art and design. Using cameras, scanners and computer software to make and manipulate digital images is an important part of design. In this book, chapters on illustrating stories and pattern show how technology can be used to extend art and design experience. Cameras are an essential tool to aid learning because children can use cameras to collect and record information quickly. Digital images can be projected for all to share or printed onto paper and used as part of the creative process. The internet offers access to limitless images, and during the projects I frequently used the web to find examples of art and design to show children. It is obviously important to check that your school has in place policies to protect children online, controlling unsupervised internet access and filtering out inappropriate material. However, from time to time children may need to search for images and ideas themselves, and teaching children how to refine and filter their search terms in order to locate relevant material is vital. Children can also experience the exciting dynamism of finding images by accident, which may generate sideways moves and out-of-the-box thinking. That said, despite the power of technology, the priority should be the feel of materials, the physical working of substances such as clay and paint to form ideas. ICT is therefore integrated into the art and design experience in this book and only used if and when it is appropriate.

Working with examples of adult art and design

Many years ago I was introduced to Rod Taylor, an advisor to schools working in Wigan. Rod talked about the 'illuminating experience' which can be a motivating concentration of attention as children are inspired through contact with original art and artists. At the Drumcroon Centre in Wigan, school children were able to work directly with examples of art and meet professional artists. The work they produced was exceptional. Visiting galleries, museums or public spaces to see art and working with artists is an essential experience for seven to eleven year olds. Of course, it is not practical to visit galleries or work with artists on every project. But in the classroom, showing children examples of the best in art and design, even if only in reproduction, is a powerful and essential part of building knowledge and understanding. For example, in Chapter 1, children were inspired by *The Wolves in the Walls,* and the powerful drawings by Dave McKean.

Opposite: this large abstract drawing is part of the pattern project (see pages 26–27)

Talking about the illustrator's work was essential to learning. This became a motivating factor in coming to understand how images and text can work together to express powerful meanings. In the same way, introducing children to appropriate paintings, sculptures, printed fabrics, and drawings should be part of a rounded experience of art and design in school.

There is a debate about whether it is best to show children examples of adult art before, during or after they make their own work. In my experience all these approaches can work well. The drawback to showing examples of art too early in a session is that children become easily influenced, thinking that this is the only way to make a painting for example, rather than trusting in their own style and approach. However, looking at how an artist applies paint before working will help children to learn more about how and why that particular technique works. For example, talking about how Van Gogh used dashes and dabs of paint in a rhythmical structure of marks across the canvas will inspire some children to create similar portraits or landscapes, which demonstrate they have understood something about how the artist generated his expressive power. The converse of this is the repetitive copying of a Van Gogh painting, so that every painting in the class looks exactly the same, without any benefits to children's individual experience and understanding.

Making art work

Finally, why is it worth spending valuable curriculum time on art and design? How is it that art is meaningful? How is design valuable? How does art and design contribute to the education of the whole child? At Dussindale Primary School, children took part in regular conversations with teachers about meta-learning. They became aware that to become better learners they should be collaborators, creative risk-takers, open minded communicators, responsive, reflective and critical thinkers. Art and design teaching and learning is a particularly valuable way to bring these, and similar values, into focus. If you read through the projects described in the chapters, you will see how these

values lie just beneath the surface of the projects and underpin the way they work.

More specific to the subject, there are a number of key concepts that underpin teaching and learning in art and design. These include: creativity which allows children to produce new and original ideas of their own; competence with a number of skills, processes, tools and materials; a growing understanding of how art and design objects express culture; and an ability to reflect critically on their own work and that of others.

For many primary teachers, it can seem as if people don't talk simply and clearly about art. It may be that during their initial teacher training comparatively little time was set aside to discuss teaching art, and in the classroom, it can sometimes be tempting either to avoid the subject or to resort to prescriptive formulas that are easy to follow. Sometimes it is only the look of the end product which dominates the planning and the making. Yet art, craft, and design surround us the whole of our lives. We should be able to talk about art in the same down-to-earth way we discuss any other human activity. Art need not be difficult or obscure activity: it touches our lives in very direct ways. Art can be demystified. The principle is to focus on the particular, individual activity rather than attempt to work in terms of general definitions and models. It is the particular nature of art that is its strength.

Art allows individual children to reach out towards the world that surrounds and is within them. Children react to this world. This reaction can be through an art activity like drawing and the drawing is their response to the world. Children feel the power of having succeeded in capturing the physical world in a physical medium. This reaction, this expression, is not abstract or esoteric, neither is it a definable system or set of slogans; it is as real as each sense of touch or sensation of smell; it is as intense as a strong colour. Children feel the power of the sensation of being alive, they are conscious of self. They are inspired to work. Art gives them this and it can be as natural, as straightforward, as rich and as particular as any of their individual words and deeds.

1

Illustrating stories

Session 1

Starting with a story

This unit of work is developed out of a literature project based upon *The Wolves in the Walls* written by Neil Gaiman and illustrated by Dave McKean. A simple PowerPoint presentation of the images can be made and used to help tell the story to the children. Projecting the images onto the whiteboard as the story is told thoroughly engages the children.

The story tells how Lucy, the chief protagonist, is sure there are wolves living in the walls of her house. Alarmingly, everybody warns that if the wolves come out of the walls, it's all over. But her family, including her cello-playing father, don't believe her. Then one day, the wolves **do** come out of the walls! The family are banished from their home. But it's not all over. Instead, Lucy rescues her special pig-puppet and finds a way of getting into the walls of her home to fight off the wolves.

Children become enthralled by Lucy and her family's predicament as they are driven out of their home by wolves. Their excitement and suspense can develop into very creative energy and straightaway, their illustrative drawing is committed.

To help children become bold and expressive in their drawing, begin with a warm up activity which explores drawing lines and making marks. You may feel it is best to do this first, before reading the story and showing the illustrations from the book.

Experimenting with lines and marks

Talk about making lines and marks. It is fun to demonstrate mark-making with the whole class. Ask everyone to sit in a circle around a large sheet of paper, or arrange an easel in front of the children with a number of large sheets of paper ready for drawing. Now encourage children to suggest words that describe how to make a mark.

Who could make a line or a mark that looks really rough? Can anyone come up and make an even rougher looking mark? Who can come up and make a line or a mark that looks really soft and gentle? Be as soft and gentle as you can. Who can come out and make a line or a mark that looks so sharp that it might cut your hand if you could grab it?

We have made lines and marks that are rough, soft and sharp. What other words can you suggest that could go with a line or mark? Every time we choose a word, one of you can come up to the easel and make a mark that might go with the word.

For example, children might suggest: short, fast, slow, lazy, jagged, pitted, tangled, bent, bold, bewildered, etc.

Another way of doing this exercise would be to ask children to suggest anything that has an interesting surface. You can collect some examples in advance: dry toast, very soft material, a bundle of thorns, rusted metal, feathers, and putty. First, ask the children to suggest words or phrases to describe the surfaces of the collection and then ask volunteers to attempt to make marks at the easel to go with the words that have been suggested. After working together, it is important to let the children experiment independently.

Now you can make a sheet of lines and marks of your own. Try out some of the ideas we talked about together and then invent new ways of making your own marks. Experiment as much as you like.

You will need: a range of drawing media for the children's own experiments; buff or off-white sugar paper, which is especially useful for charcoal, chalk and soft pastels; large sheets of paper; an easel or flip chart; marker pens; drawing boards; odourless hair spray to fix any experiments with media that may smudge.

Opposite: it is tempting to see this as scribbling but in fact this is careful and considered work by these boys. They were able to use these sheets as part of their large wolf collages later in the project

Right: exploring how lines and marks might be used to create the rough, bristly, hairy coat of a wolf. It helps to build confidence if children are encouraged to work on a large scale. Working collaboratively helps break down inhibitions, particularly if some children feel anxious about their work. This is all about experimenting and exploring

Right: wolf drawing

Session 2

Talking about wolves

Read again to children extracts from the story that describe the wolves and what they are like. Children can continue in an entirely imaginative way without looking at illustrations or images of wolves. However, it is also a valuable strategy to show and talk about images and video extracts of real wolves and then compare these with illustrations from the book.

You can list all the features of wolves (sharp teeth, pointed ears, wild eyes, etc.) and talk about the visual qualities of wolves. Link this conversation back to some of the vocabulary you used when making the line and mark experiments. Do not show the children the illustrations in the book again at this stage. It is a richer activity, if they come up with visual ideas themselves.

If you could touch a wolf, what would it be like? What would the wolf's hair be like? What about its head? What would you feel if you could touch a wolf's head?

Drawing wolves

Invite children to explore their ideas by drawing only certain parts of wolves. For example, they could draw wolf eyes, teeth, ears, heads, claws, etc. Children could also make a digital collection of images of wolves. If they can crop digital images, they could make a scrapbook-style collection of bits of wolves that they think might be useful. Afterwards, children can begin to draw their own versions of imaginary wolves to illustrate the story. What moment from the story should the children illustrate? They may choose the point where the wolves first come out of the walls; but there are other dramatic moments full of action.

You are each going to have a large sheet of paper to make your own imaginary wolf drawings. There is no need to draw all of the wolf. It may be best just to draw the body or even just his head and shoulders. It's up to you.

Most important is to remember that you can use the drawing media in many different ways to make different kinds of marks. You may want to experiment again before you make your large drawing. For example, you might want to try out different ways of showing what you think the wolf's coat would be like if you could feel it. You have a large sheet of paper, so think big! You can draw more than one wolf! Remember these are imaginary wolves. The illustrator, Dave McKean, drew his wolves so that we really can feel how scary it would be if a pack of wolves suddenly jumped out of the walls of your house!

You will need: drawing media – strong, bold lines and marks have a graphic power so it is best to avoid, for example, HB pencils; large sheets of paper; drawing boards; masking tape; hair spray if children are using charcoal, chalk and soft pastels; sketchbooks; *The Wolves in the Walls*.

Each of the four remaining pictures show eight-year-old children working on their imaginative wolf drawings to illustrate Neil Gaiman's story. The wolf coat line and mark experiments have been torn up to use for collage if needed. Children could also cut out and use some of the wolf parts which they have already drawn

Having an exhibition

If children have been drawing on paper attached to their drawing boards with masking tape, it is easy to mount a quick exhibition. Prop up the finished drawings along the wall of the corridor or in the school hall. We left all the large drawings flat on the tables and children circulated around the class looking at each other's work. Ask children to choose their favourite wolf or wolves. Ask them for reasons for their choices. Ask them who drew the most fearsome wolf! Compare different styles of drawing – for example, some children will have been more careful about the details, others more original and daring in the way they drew the wolf. An issue here is the question: what are children looking for when they choose their favourite drawings? How do we choose what we like? One objective of this session is to help children to be more careful and thoughtful about the judgments they make about what they think is a 'good' drawing. There is no reason why children cannot become aware of some of the values that underpin their individual taste for one style of work or another.

Looking at the book illustrations

Make a connection again to the illustrations in the book. Ask the children to compare their own illustrations with those in the book. Which do they prefer? Why? How are the illustrations in the book different from their own? How could they make their own drawings smaller to fit inside a real book?

Session 3

Working with digital imagery

Children will be excited to see their large-scale wolf drawings emerge. But how could they develop them into illustrations in a book? Digitising their hand-drawn images offers many opportunities for further work, and it is very possible to aim at printing or presenting an illustrated story.

First of all, children should take photographs of their drawings with a digital camera. They will have to work out how best to do this. They could pin the drawings to a vertical surface or perhaps lay them flat on the floor and attempt to take a photograph looking directly down at the image. Talk with children about available light and remind them that the images will look brighter if the light is good. They can experiment to see what difference flash will make.

The photographs of the drawings will need to be transferred to a computer. Once saved, there are a number of basic photo editing tools which children can use. Images can be enlarged, reduced or even cropped, so that only one part of the original drawing is used. Various effects and colours can be applied. Most importantly, text can be added to the image.

Make a bank of the kind of vocabulary, phrases or sentences which could be useful. Look at the use of text in *The Wolves in the Walls*. Talk about how the font, size and positioning of the text will all make a

difference to how the page looks and reads. Are there any special effects? Is any bit of text more important?

During our project, several children decided to use their knowledge of PowerPoint to make a series of images with animated text and sound. As well as adding text, they recorded words and phrases to be saved and added to the PowerPoint. These could be activated as each slide was shown. Children in this class were also familiar with Photo Story software. However, software for manipulating and presenting digital images suitable for children is being developed and improved all the time.

You will need: a camera or scanner; computer and software for manipulating images and adding text to images; access to printer.

Opposite: children cut out their wolf drawings and glued them onto black paper before taking photographs. Text can be added to these large graphic works for display in the classroom

Right and above: children worked in pairs to create their own illustrations for The Wolves in the Walls. *They talked about text they would like to add. Some chose to work in PowerPoint and create a narrative series of slides (or pages). This boy chose to paste images of jam into his wolf drawing, having decided that his wolves were coming out of the walls to steal jam!*

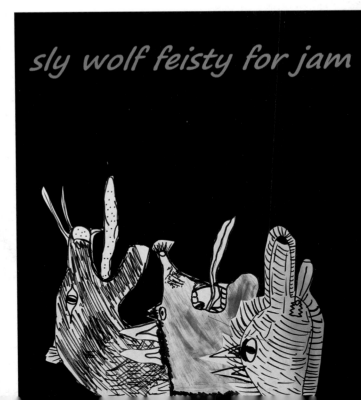

Session 4

Talking to a graphic designer and book illustrator

A school visit from an illustrator or graphic designer would greatly enhance children's understanding of how a book is illustrated and designed as they could show children something of the creative processes involved. An illustrator might describe reading the manuscript, using a sketchbook or a computer to research ideas, making a storyboard to check that the story fits properly into the book, preliminary drawings and sketches, and then developing the final artwork. For example, during a school visit, an illustrator told how he used a special textured paper for water colour. He explained that the particular texture of the paper affected the look of his drawings. The class teacher was able to reinforce the idea that the choice of materials will affect the look of the finished product. This sparked a discussion by children about the advantages and disadvantages of using different media such as charcoal, HB pencils or paint for an illustration.

There should be many different examples of book illustration in a school library. It is also possible to look for work by illustrators online. However, there is nothing better than having the opportunity to look through a portfolio of work with an adult illustrator who can answer questions and offer numerous insights into how he or she works.

Identifying stories or books to illustrate

You can help children discover that there are different types of illustrations appropriate to different kinds of books. In the library, the children found illustrations for bible stories, cartoons, imaginative stories, history books, graphic novels and geography books, as well as all kinds of non-fiction books and reference books. They discussed possible stories or books which might be good to use as starting points for their own illustrations. Children will also be able to illustrate their own stories and create stories which, as in the case of *The Wolves in the Walls*, depend on illustrations for much of the narrative content.

Researching ideas

Children should make a collection of digital images as a way of researching visual material that might be useful. For example, if a drawing of a castle is appropriate for a story, then a child could be encouraged to use the internet or library to find images of different castles. A useful image can be used for inspiration. Any source of visual material might be used to help develop an illustration.

Top left: working together on elements of a story on separate sheets of paper

Top right: assembling the story sections (could be paragraphs or chapters) into a strip

Making story strips

The photographs show children making story strips, which is a simple way of creating a story board. Having decided on a story to illustrate, children are given strips of paper. These can be folded or divided into a given number of sections by a teacher, or the children can work more freely, deciding how to divide up the strip themselves. They could even work on separate, similar-sized pieces of paper which they attach together. If the story extends beyond the strip, a new section can be added. The strips can become like scrolls. Children can both write and draw the critical elements which they wish to illustrate. Talk about the balance between text and image. Which do they feel should dominate at any point in the story? Remind children that text can be placed in different ways in relation to the image. These story strips can make excellent planning tools for creating well-structured narratives. In this class, we used them as cue cards to help children tell their stories. These were recorded. Children improved their oral storytelling by listening to the recordings and repeating the tale again, after thinking and talking about how to enhance the story.

You will need: strips of paper, drawing media

2

Using pattern

Session 1

Talking about patterns

It is always helpful to talk about general characteristics of pattern, even if children are older. More demanding pattern questions and challenges can be set for more advanced children.

Who is wearing a pattern? Can you show us? Who is wearing a pattern of lines? Who is wearing a pattern of shapes? Who is wearing a pattern of colours? What is the difference between a pattern and a picture? A pattern must have something that repeats itself a number of times. What can you see in the classroom that has parts that repeat again and again? Where can you see patterns in the classroom?

Collecting patterns from home, school and the internet

Ask the children to bring in items from home that have pattern. Talk about the possibilities: fabric off-cuts, wallpaper, items of clothing, bags and boxes, food packaging, decorative items of all kinds. Make a display with the collected objects. Enhance the collection with patterns found in school. An internet image search for pattern will produce a wealth of examples. Try augmenting the search with terms such as: natural pattern, animal pattern, floral pattern, Victorian pattern, Celtic pattern, crystal pattern, geometric pattern. There is a wealth of other possibilities! Pattern images can be printed or collected as digital media in folders.

Collecting together ideas of all kinds is a useful tool for many creative activities. If it is appropriate, talk with children about how they might make their own collection of patterns. For example, a camera might be useful, or scissors and glue to help make a collage of patterns. They could make their own collections of digital images in personal folders on a computer. A traditional way is to ask the children to collect some examples of the patterns they have found by drawing in sketchbooks or on single sheets of paper. Remind them that there is no need to draw all of the object which has a pattern. They only need to draw enough to show clearly that it has a pattern. Children could also use a viewfinder (a small window cut in a sheet of paper or card) to isolate small areas of pattern.

You might decide to structure this activity further by asking children to collect only one category of pattern, for example, a collection of natural patterns. In this case, magnifying glasses and a digital microscope might be useful, as well as cameras and internet image searches. Enlarge the patterns for display, or make photocopies and printouts as material that children can select and then use for collages. As before, children can draw the natural patterns in their sketchbooks. Patterns can also be collected by making rubbings.

You will need: sketchbooks or paper; drawing media; viewfinder; digital cameras; computers and a connection to the internet; photocopier; magnifying glasses; digital microscope.

Top left: drawing examples of patterns from a selection of printouts made from a collection of digital images of pattern. Notice how the girl on the right is using a viewfinder to isolate part of a pattern

Top right: making an informal exhibition of work by laying out the drawings on table tops and inviting children to view each one. There will be many talking points

Right: making pattern collections in a sketchbook. This eight year old collected patterns from the classroom first and is now designing a pattern of her own

Session 2

Researching patterns from other cultures

Ask the children's parents if they can lend the class any patterns that are special to their culture, religion or country of origin. Are there any fabrics, items of clothing or decorative objects that can be borrowed? Are there any photographs, printouts or books that can be used in a display?

If you visit local places of worship you may be able to find some examples of patterns that are linked with a specific religion or cultural identity. The school library and the internet will also be a rich source of patterns from many different parts of the world. Ask the children to see what they can find. Museums can be an excellent source of different patterns collected from different cultures. It is possible to buy cheaply-priced postcards and books that will provide paper-based resources for projects such as this for many years. Try your local museum; perhaps the curator or education officer may help. One of the delights of this work is the richness and variety of pattern-making. A sumptuous and exciting display of pattern will feed the children's own art for many weeks.

Collecting examples of patterns from different parts of the world

Ask the children to make their own collection of patterns from other cultures. You could decide to theme this, particularly if it is appropriate to learning in other areas of the curriculum. For example, collecting patterns from the Islamic world could be an important part of understanding Islamic culture and part of a study of Islamic religion. Again, if children are drawing patterns, a viewfinder might help them focus on a particular part of a pattern, as there is no need for them to draw the whole of a patterned object or image. They may wish to draw or make collages from printed material, or make digital collections using a computer. Try scanning patterns. Children can then explore the possibilities of colouring, cutting, pasting, moving and printing the stored patterns.

You will need: sketchbook or paper; drawing media; viewfinder; digital cameras; computers and a connection to the internet; photocopier; and examples of patterns from other cultures.

Above: this school made a collection of patterned objects from all over the world. Children are using sketchbooks to collect pattern ideas

Session 3

Designing a pattern

Out of all the patterns you have seen, which is your favourite? Choose a part of that pattern, a shape, for example, or perhaps a line. Use the shape or line as part of a new pattern of your own. Think up some ideas and try them out first. When you are sure you know what you want the design of your pattern to look like, use the smaller pieces of paper and draw your pattern out to fill the whole sheet. Make sure the pattern goes right up to all four sides of the paper. Use colour as well. Don't forget that the way colours repeat in your design can be a vital feature of your pattern.

A more prescriptive but also more focused approach would be to limit the children to using motifs from one culture. This would mean that their pattern had the character of, say, an Islamic or Celtic pattern.

You will need: sketchbooks or paper; drawing media; small sheets of paper.

Above and right: designing patterns inspired by patterns from cultures around the world

Session 4

Applying the pattern designs

Children can apply patterns they have designed in numerous ways. The photographs illustrate how this class developed their pattern ideas collaboratively. Firstly, children talked about their pattern collections. You can help children become more aware of the different qualities of various patterns. For example, patterns may be regular, geometric, complex, irregular, bold, delicate, or simple. Patterns might be entirely abstract, or made from recognisable motifs such as flowers, animals or stars. Some patterns are used in very deliberate and precise ways as part of an object's decoration. Others are simply seen across the entire surface of something – a floor covering, or curtain fabric, for example.

Secondly, children were given large sheets of paper covering two rectangular tabletops. They worked in small groups to decide which of all their pattern ideas could be used and combined to create a large abstract drawing based on the concept of pattern. Some children made rough plans before they began work on the large sheets. Working together, children began to fill the large sheets with pattern ideas to create their abstract drawings. Finally, children reviewed and talked about their work. It is exciting to work on a large scale. This type of art project is a useful way of building an understanding of qualities children will need to develop to be successful learners in all areas of the curriculum. These include: being risk takers, working collaboratively as part of a team, and thinking outside the box in a creative way.

Other ideas for pattern designs

The children could use their pattern to decorate a plate. A more complex idea is to use a mould technique. Use an enamel or hard plastic bowl or plate as a base and cover it with a film of margarine. Then apply three layers of torn tissue paper coated in wallpaper or cold water starch paste. The margarine will make it possible for the hardened tissue paper to be removed easily from the plate. While the paste is still wet, add a final layer of tissue. The wallpaper paste will allow the children to smooth the tissue onto the form of the plate or bowl. This final layer can be a pattern of colours and shapes and the children can choose different colours. Children could also create a pattern by adding a variety of different media and materials. They might use string, metallic papers, wool, thin fabric shapes, coloured shapes or fragments of paper that they have decorated with a pattern of their own.

Buy a paper linen-effect tablecloth from a supermarket. Use large felt pens to draw out one design or perhaps a number of the children's individual designs. Children will need to think big.

Use strips of white fabric so that the children can apply their patterns to make headbands, scarves or ties. Use fabric crayons or paints.

Remind the children how to print using polystyrene tiles. Or look ahead to page 108 and the advice about block printing. Ask them to transfer their pattern to a tile and then print the design. They could use their pattern as a motif for a greetings card or gift wrapping paper.

Top left: planning how to go about starting a large drawing

Top right: reviewing work at appropriate intervals. Here children are beginning to talk about the colours they might use

Ask the children to suggest other things that might be decorated with their pattern. Whether the children go on to work on plates, fabric or make prints, the key to this unit of work is the successful application of a design. The complication for primary school children is that the process and media used will affect the kind of pattern that can be applied. For example, shapes cut from tissue paper may not be the best way of making a complex pattern inspired by Celtic knots. Older children aged nine to eleven could be challenged to design a pattern appropriate to the process that they will be using to make or decorate their artefact. Equally, they may be challenged to devise a process appropriate to a pattern they had previously designed.

Top left: using a limited range of colours. These are soft pastels. Children tested and selected their colours before starting work

Top right and above: these abstract drawings soon took on a life of their own because children had a rich collection of pattern ideas before starting their work

Session 5

Applying pattern designs using digital technology

It is important for children to investigate and develop ideas before they create computer-generated designs – in fact it is vital, as it is all too easy to produce facile and rather crude patterns using a computer. Look back at the previous sessions in this chapter about how children can research, collect and develop visual ideas. Other ideas for source material that might inspire new computer-aided design include: geometric designs found in architecture, woven textiles, bead work, masks, and ceramic decoration from a variety of countries and cultures.

Images can be edited, altered and worked, once the original image has been saved. Encourage children to save their designs regularly, to avoid the disappointment of losing them. Areas of a drawn picture or shape can be filled with different colours and the colour combinations changed at will. Geometric shapes such as squares, rectangles and triangles can be manipulated by reflection or rotation on screen. Images can be enlarged and reduced in size.

Many programmes have facilities so that children can explore different ways of manipulating an image on the screen. They can reposition images and then repeat small areas of a pattern or motif again and again. This links well to designing wallpaper, wrapping paper and printed textiles. You can use any draw or paint software package. The tools may include the option to draw freehand or geometrically, using a range of brush sizes and colours. Children can also work with existing images that have been scanned. Computer-generated images can be used for many purposes. Remember that the computer is an essential tool in graphic design and children should be comfortable using it in this way.

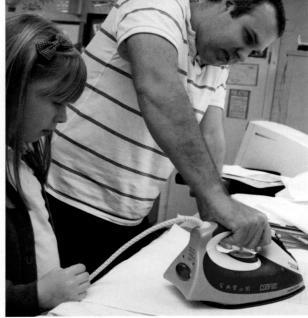

Transferring images from computer to fabric

Technology can be applied to almost any design project, as these photographs show. Children used a technique for transferring designs from the computer to fabric, scanning various pattern designs of their own. They printed these onto special heat-sensitive paper, which with adult help can be used to transfer designs directly onto fabric using a domestic iron. The children explored what happens when the same printed paper image is used several times. Each time the image is ironed onto a new piece of fabric, it lightens in colour.

Why not use this process to print designs on T-shirts? This could become part of a mini-enterprise project. The cost of materials and blank T-shirts can be calculated. The clothing products should incorporate original designs and could be sold to family and friends.

The children in the photographs transferred the designs onto a long band of fabric which could be used as part of a ceremonial costume. For example, it could be folded like a turban and worn on the head, used like a scarf, draped over the shoulders rather like a stole, or worn as a sash.

Another group suggested using colour printouts to make jewellery. The colour printouts are glued onto thin card and the children cut the card into many different shapes. The children used a hole punch and threaded these shapes onto coloured raffia to make wrist bands, anklets and necklaces. Other children made earrings or brooches. One child remembered that the school had a laminator and asked if was practical to laminate her

card shapes. Another boy worked out that he could use PVA glue to give his patterned jewellery a glossy finish.

You can show children how to roll and glue tight tubes of paper with their designs on. These can be sliced into macaroni-like beads. Different lengths of tubes can be joined in various ways to create larger items of jewellery and body adornments.

The project might continue in various ways:

You have different examples of patterns saved on the computer. Can you think up other ways of using the printouts of your patterns to create jewellery and body adornments? Work in groups to 'brainstorm' a number of ideas. Don't forget to think about what tools or materials you will need. We will share the ideas you develop and talk about the practical problems involved in trying them out.

You will need: printouts of designs; heat sensitive transfer paper; card; PVA and other paper glues; scissors; hole punch; raffia string, ribbons and wools; a domestic iron (to be used by an adult); access to a scanner and printer.

Top left: using the computer to transfer photographed or scanned designs to heat sensitive paper

Top right: an adult should help iron the back of the heat-sensitive paper to transfer the design on to fabric

Right: peeling off the backing paper to reveal the design

Opposite: wearing ceremonial costumes inspired by their work with patterns

3

Forests

Session 1

An indoor forest

Collect together different houseplants from around the school and invite children to bring them in from home. It is best to have a number of plants of different sizes and with different kinds of leaves. The more plants you find, the larger and more exciting will be the indoor forest that you create in the classroom. You could make the forest on a circular table in the centre of the room, with plants on top of, underneath, and on the floor around the table. The effect is of a confusion of different greenery. After the initial set of activities, the indoor forest can be moved to make a display at the side of the classroom.

Focusing on shape

The first exercise is a warm up, revision exercise designed to help children focus on one of the visual qualities, shape. Refer to pages 76 and 77 where an introduction to shape is described in full. If children have not worked in this way before, or if basic work on shape needs revising, start the project with a suitable version of the activities described on pages 76 and 77. Even if children are experienced young artists, it is always worth devising a simple warm-up exercise to help them re-focus on a relevant visual quality.

Give children drawing media such as felt-tips, handwriting pens or black wax crayons so they will not be able to rub out their shape drawings. Look at pages 62 and 63 for a discussion about how to build children's confidence so they can draw without worrying too much about making mistakes.

Collecting leaf shapes from the indoor forest

Children should now find it easy to move on to collecting all the different leaf shapes they can find in the indoor forest.

Look at the leaves in the indoor forest. What are some of the differences between the shapes of the leaves? Look at this leaf. How would you describe its shape? Here is another leaf that looks completely different from the first one. What words would you use to describe its shape?

Right: collecting leaf shapes using drawing boards and soft drawing pencils

Below: it is important that children change position from time to time. Remind them that each individual leaf will have a different shape depending on the angle of view

Use your paper and drawing boards to collect the different shapes of the leaves in the indoor forest. Try to show the special shape that each leaf has. Even leaves from the same plant may have very different shapes. Try to show that the leaf shapes have different sizes, some may look quite large on the page, and others may be very small. But don't make all your drawings too tiny! The shape of a leaf will change depending on your viewpoint. Try drawing the same leaf from different positions. There is no need to put in all the detail you can see on each leaf.

It isn't necessary to be too strict about drawing in detail. Some children will enjoy showing all the veins and patterns visible in each leaf, but they should be collecting a number of different examples and not spending too much time on one drawing. You may need to emphasise that children should draw only the leaves and not the whole plant. You could easily extend this exercise by asking children to collect examples of leaf shapes from the environment around the school.

You will need: drawing media; sketchbooks or drawing boards and paper; an indoor forest of houseplants.

Session 2

Talking about Rousseau's painting, *Surprised!*

A good way to begin the forest project would be to discuss this painting. You could use any painting or drawing that shows a variety of leaves. Another option would be to show children fabrics with a leaf motif design. This latter choice would be particularly appropriate if you were thinking of making fabric design one of the outcomes of the project.

Children could be asked to list everything they see in the painting. They could then discuss the different shapes of the leaves that Rousseau has painted and the shapes of some of the other images, particularly the shape of the tiger, including its teeth and tail. The foliage shows a variety of different greens. Children can comment on the differences in the shades of green used to show the leaves. You could go on to ask the class what they thought was happening in the painting. What is the tiger doing? What is the tiger feeling? How would they feel if they were in the painting?

What was going to happen next? You could ask the children about their opinions of Rousseau's painting. What did they like about it? What did they dislike? Would they put the painting up at home to look at every day? If not, why not?

Practical activities following the discussion

Children could collect different examples of leaf shapes from Rousseau's painting. They could also try mixing the variety of different greens that Rousseau used.

You will need: Rousseau's painting *Surprised!* or any other forest painting; an alternative is a collection of fabrics with flora and fauna motifs; sketchbooks or drawing boards and paper; drawing media; hairspray; soft pastels, or all the equipment for mixing colours in paint (ready-mix paint; containers for different colours; mixing palettes; water in containers; different-sized brushes; rags or sponges).

Top: Surprised! *by Henri Rousseau, 1891, Bought, with the aid of a substantial donation from the Hon. Walter H. Annenberg, 1972 © The National Gallery, London, NG6421*

Right: Talking about another Rousseau painting – sometimes using posters is better than projecting images on a whiteboard as the children can see all the colours the artist used

Session 3

Making observational or imaginative forest drawings

An alternative at this stage would be to ask children to make a straightforward observational drawing of the indoor forest. You could set the children up to draw with drawing boards and paper. Ask them to focus on shape. They could use a viewfinder to help focus on a section of the indoor forest (look at page 22 for advice on using viewfinders). However, it might be more appropriate for the class to use their initial investigations and the stimulus of the houseplant collection to make an imaginative, rather than a strictly observational response.

You are going to use the drawing boards and some paper to make an imaginative forest drawing of your own. You will need to be able to see our indoor forest whilst you work but you do not need to copy it exactly. You will need your first leaf drawings beside you. You can look at these and use ideas from them whenever you like. You can make your forest drawing in any way you choose but here are a few things I would like you to think about.

Draw lots of different kinds of leaves; give them different shapes and sizes. The leaves in our indoor forest and in Rousseau's painting overlap one on top of another. You should draw your forest leaves overlapping or covering each other.

Children may need help to grasp the practical implications of the concept of overlapping. If this is the case, it may first be appropriate to design an activity that allows the class to experiment with overlapping shapes. For example, ask children to collect different leaf shapes, only instead of drawing each leaf separately on the page, ask them to draw the shape of each new leaf overlapping one they have already collected.

Start drawing the leaves in the middle of your paper and work slowly towards the sides, the top and the bottom of the paper. You are using a felt-tip pen or black wax crayon so you can't rub out bits you don't like. So there is no point worrying about mistakes, everybody will make them. Just keep going.

The children will want to add animals to their drawings. It will help them to make a library search and collect in the classroom or library area books with illustrations of animals that live in the rainforest. They could also search the internet and make a collection of appropriate digital images of animal shapes.

Make some simple drawings to show the different shapes of some of the animals that live in forests, especially rainforests. Can you tell what kind of animal you were looking at from the shape you have drawn?

At this point, it is worth looking at the advice about drawing shapes on pages 76 and 77. You can organise children into different groups to collect different categories of animals. Or you could simply make sure that each group collects at least one bird, insect, mammal, reptile, etc. Some children will gain confidence if they are allowed to trace the animal shape first.

Draw lots of the forest before you start putting in any animals. You can look at our indoor forest and copy the leaves if you find that helpful. Don't draw the pots. There are no plant pots in a real forest.

Look at some of the books from the library again, if there are any other animals that you didn't collect first time around. You can look at Rousseau's painting for ideas, but do not copy the painting. This is a forest drawing of your own.

Left: this girl has used all the space on her paper and is well on the way to creating her own imaginative forest drawing

Below: starting a drawing in colour. Look out for and give lots of positive reinforcement for imaginative ideas such as the yellow and black leaves or fruit

This work is not necessarily in colour. Line drawings can be very graphic and exciting without adding colour. However, colour could easily become a feature of the project not only by concentrating on the range of different greens, but also by looking at the exotic colours of some forest birds and animals.

Some children do not find it easy to visualise how to compose a drawing that will fit into the space of the paper. For example, some children will make very small drawings; others will draw along a narrow strip at the bottom of the paper. In this project, it will help to suggest to children that they should start in the middle of the paper and then spread out the drawing from the centre towards the edges. Children will feel more confident about where to start; and they are therefore more likely to draw fluently, naturally filling the paper with their drawing. However, this is only one compositional device and there are many other ways to set about composing a drawing. The point of using this approach is to simplify the problem of composition for children. They already have more than enough to think about as they concentrate on shapes, overlapping, and so on.

Talking about the finished drawings

The children will learn a lot by looking at each other's work and by being asked to comment on what they like and admire. Leave the drawings fixed to the drawing boards and have an exhibition, propping the boards up along a wall.

You will need: drawing boards and paper; drawing media; masking tape or clips; the indoor forest (this project works best if children are able to make their own drawings with the atmosphere of the plant collection around them); Rousseau's painting or other examples of art, craft and design with a forest theme; a collection of books with photographs or illustrations of rainforest animals; examples of animal shapes sourced via the internet.

Left: adding colours and patterns to sheets of sugar paper in different ways to provide a rich variety of papers to use in the collage

Session 4

Developing the forest project: making a paper collage

There are many ways to develop the forest theme. For example, the basic investigative and imaginative work could inform work in clay, paint, collage, printing, design, and sculptural construction. On page 38 is an example of collage work that could be developed from the work done so far. Collage naturally involves possibilities for overlapping shapes, a theme that emerged in the earlier drawing sessions.

Apart from the forest theme, the technique of making a paper collage can be adapted for many different themes, topics or starting points.

Children could work on ornamental designs for their collages. There are many fabric designs that have tropical or exotic plants as an underlying theme. Find some examples to show the children. This work could be linked to developing pattern-based designs from the previous chapter.

There is no doubt that the specific examples of relevant art and design that you discuss with the class will deeply affect decisions they make in their own work. For example, children could look at extracts from Walt Disney's *Jungle Book* and it might be possible to use other short video extracts from films that feature the rainforest. Looking at Disney's film could become the start of a different project which involves drawing and cutting out animal and plant shapes. If the work is extended in this way, children could discover how to make legs, heads and tails move. The children might then make flat bed two-dimensional animation. (This is when the camera is pointed down at a horizontal flat background onto which two-dimensional shapes and images are manipulated to create the appearance of movement). You could show children how they can animate a two-dimensional forest scene by using a video camera with an animation facility linked to appropriate software. In this way, the forest theme could progress in a number of different directions; but here is an account of how to develop a forest collage project.

Colouring sugar papers

Coloured sugar paper is usually available in school and it is inexpensive; however, the colours are not very exciting. Forests are rich in colour; particularly a rich variety of greens. This first process is designed to enable children to create their own coloured papers for a collaborative forest collage.

The children will need plenty of different coloured sugar paper. Ask them to use soft pastels and to experiment with different ways of applying new colour to the paper.

Can you think up different ways of using the pastels? How about using the side, pressing hard or pressing softly? Can you think up ways of making marks to make patterned effects? How many different colours could you use? We could add at least two new colours to the sugar paper. What happens when you put one colour on top of another? Are there other ways you could combine the colours? There are many different ways that you could colour the paper.

As it is a forest collage, you could ask the children to make many sheets of different greens. This task can be linked to the investigation of the different greens they discovered in the leaves of the houseplants, or to an exploration of greens in the landscape, prior to making a landscape drawing or painting (see page 41). Or, they could make a forest of fantastical colours. Not only leaves, but forest flowers, fruits, birds and animals will need a different range of colours. There is great potential here for rich and varied mark- and pattern-making.

The sheets of coloured papers will need to be sprayed with hairspray to prevent too much dust and smudging before the children move on to the next stage. There are other possibilities for making a resource bank of different coloured papers for use in a collage. Try using other materials and techniques to colour the papers. For example, more confident children could be given a choice of pastels, paint, inks, marbling equipment and diffusion sprays. In fact, this session could focus on experimenting with how different materials create different effects.

You will need: sheets of different-coloured sugar paper; soft pastels (you can use coloured chalks but pastels have particularly strong colours. Children could also use paint, inks, marbling techniques); hairspray; a box or drawer to store the coloured sheets; polythene to cover the tables as this session is messy!

Tearing and cutting leaf shapes

You can use scissors or tear the leaf shapes. Look at all the different leaf shapes you collected. Look at all the different leaves in our indoor forest. Look at the leaf shapes in Rousseau's painting. Remember how different one shape is from another. You said that some are large, some are small, some are pointed, some are rounded, some are thin, some shapes are repeated again and again and some are complicated. So remember to make a variety of different shapes and sizes of leaves. As you work, store the finished leaf shapes carefully.

You will need: pre-coloured sheets of paper; scissors; somewhere to store all the paper leaves.

Above and right: cutting out a variety of shapes to use in the collage. These children began by cutting out different sizes and shapes of forest leaves

Session 5

Making the collage

In this project, children worked in groups and pooled the coloured papers and then the leaf shapes. Each group made their own large collage. However, children could work on individual collages, or perhaps the whole class could become involved in making one shared end product.

Adding animals and flowers

Children will want to add animals to the collage. They may also want to add other things such as fruit, flowers, even forest people. The collage may be entirely imaginary. To prepare for this, follow the steps described in *Colouring sugar papers* on page 35, but make colours and shapes of imaginary animals, fruit and people as well as leaves.

Children may find it helpful to trace the shapes of animals and then transfer the traced images to the back of the pre-coloured sugar paper. After all, a designer would not hesitate to use computer technology to collect relevant animal shapes. A child-friendly version of this would be to print out animal shapes and glue them onto the back of pre-coloured sugar papers. Children can use these as a template to cut out the shape. Children could go on to make cardboard stencils which will be useful for drawing around to repeat the same shape many times.

There are aesthetic and practical choices to be made here. Older and more advanced children will have the knowledge and experience needed to make informed judgements about the approach they wish to adopt. If you can show children that there are a number of different possibilities, they will take creative control over the work. In practice this has to be balanced with the pressure of the often limited time available for art and the need to ensure effective and workable classroom management.

Composing the collage and starting to glue

If children want their animals peering out from behind leaves, they will need to plan for this before they glue down many leaf shapes.

There are many ways that you could arrange your shapes on the paper to compose the collage. Where would you like to start on the paper? Is it best to start with small leaves or larger leaves? How will the animals fit in? What will you need to do if you have too many shapes for the size of paper? Can your collage have too much in it? Choose some of the shapes you like and start arranging them on this large sheet of paper. Don't forget the shapes can overlap. When you are satisfied, begin to glue the shapes carefully on the paper. Remember this 'How to' method to help you glue without getting in a mess:

- *Your working area is divided into two with a strip of masking tape.*
- *Keep a clean side of the area for your collage.*
- *The glue spreader, glue, sponges for sticky fingers and newspaper always stay on the dirty side of the area.*
- *Always use glue on a clean sheet of newspaper, so put a new sheet of newspaper down on the gluing side every time you glue a new shape. If you have an old magazine to glue on, turn a page each time you glue a new shape, then you won't get glue on everything.*
- *Don't use too much glue. If it squeezes out from underneath the paper when you press the shape down on the collage, you have used too much.*
- *Glue over the edges so that the paper shapes stick flat. Use the sponge to wipe glue off your fingers and any small drops that fall on the collage or the table. Glue will go over the edges of your paper shape onto the newspaper. That's why you put a*

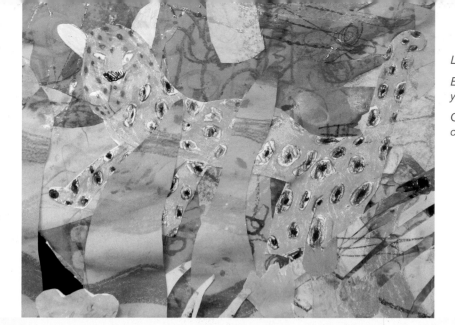

new sheet of newspaper down on the gluing side of the area every time you glue a new shape!
- *If you are working as a group, why not organise yourselves into a team so that different children have different jobs to do?*

Some groups will find the task of arranging the leaf shapes for their collage and then gluing them down difficult, since it is the leaf shapes nearest the paper that need to be glued down first. This means that the arrangement will need to be disturbed before it can be glued down permanently. Encourage children to think about this problem and suggest solutions. However, in the midst of a creative project such as this, children will simply become lost in the moment as they make their artwork. It is sometimes more harmful to insist on a rigid structure for the work than to allow a certain amount of apparent chaos. When to intervene (with the danger of prescription and taking creative control away from children), and when to let the work flow independently

(and so risking muddle, confusion and mess), is a judgement call which the teacher has to make.

You will need: polythene to cover tables; masking tape to mark out clean and dirty areas; PVA glue; glue containers; glue spreaders; damp sponges or rags; scissors; coloured paper shapes with which to make the collage.

Finishing the collage

Children can add drawn elements onto the collaged paper shapes. They might use pastels to add large areas of colour (such as the sky). Some children will be inspired to make individual collages. Is there a way to challenge able children to explore collage technique in more depth? Look at examples of photomontage in art and design for inspiration and ideas.

4

Landscape drawing and painting

Session 1

Starting points

Here are some suggestions for starting work on landscape. The idea is to choose one or more of the visual qualities as a focus for landscape drawing and painting. These might include shape, colour, tone, space, line and texture. This approach may be adapted to work with almost any subject. If the children have recently worked with an appropriate visual quality (for example, they may have been working with shape for the forest project in Chapter 3), there will be no need to repeat some of the experimental work. However, it is too easy to undervalue the benefit of simple warm-up exercises. Try to find some way of allowing children to explore, experiment and investigate before expecting them to produce finished artwork. If children have previously worked from landscape using ideas about shape as a focus, choose a new starting point which focuses on a visual quality that suggests a different way of looking at the subject. This session suggests six of the visual qualities as a possible starting point. You only need to choose one or two for children to find a real visual focus to begin drawing landscape.

Starting with shape

Look at the work described on pages 76 and 77. This could be used to prepare children before they begin drawing a landscape. Ask the children to use their sketchbooks to collect some of the different shapes they can see in the landscape. The shapes of fields, trees, bushes, houses, clouds, hills, pylons, factories, sheds, cranes. This works well for rural, semi-rural, urban or industrial landscapes.

You will need: sketchbooks or drawing boards and paper; drawing media (use anything which makes clear lines. The aim is to build children's confidence whilst drawing, so use media which cannot be rubbed out easily).

Starting with colour, using pastels

If children worked through the forest project, they may well have investigated mixing a range of greens with the soft pastels. Exploring different greens is a useful starting point for landscape work in pastel. However, if they have already experimented with different greens, why not take the children outside and ask them to explore some of the other colours that make up the landscape? If they are experimenting, remind them that there is no need to draw pictures, patches of colour are fine: it is only the colours that are important. The idea here is that the children should attempt to mix the kinds of colours they can see. This can be a difficult task. Give children two chances to find appropriate colours. First, encourage them to experiment without worrying about making the colours too accurate. They will find many appropriate colours by accident. Second time around, ask children to be more precise and only record colours that they can find in the landscape. Ask children to think of ways of describing or naming the colours they have created and observed.

You will need: sketchbooks or drawing boards and paper; pastels (both oil and soft pastels could be used); hairspray to fix the soft pastel experiments.

Starting with colour, using paint

The same activity could be undertaken using paint. Colour-mixing is a basic skill that children can learn and practise before they are seven. A summary of the technique can be found on page 48. In good weather, it is possible for children to take the equipment they need and paint outside; or they could use paint to recreate some of the landscape colours they discovered using pastels. Their work should still be experimental, and they should not be trying to paint pictures. The children could simply make a lot of patches of colour on white paper.

Top: exploring and experimenting by mixing greens with pastels

Above: as a starter activity these children are beginning to collect shapes in the classroom before going outside to draw. This same activity can be used with five year olds; however this kind of warm up is very valuable for nine and ten year olds. Notice how drawing boards provide flexible and mobile work surfaces

Other ways of exploring colour

Children could search for landscape colours in colour supplements and magazines. They could cut out fragments of colour and collage colour collections onto paper. The children might continue by matching some of the colours they found with paint they mixed for themselves.

You may wish to link this work with simple colour theory. Are the children familiar with the colour wheel? Children should already know about primary and secondary colours. Do they know how to make browns, tertiary colours? Children could be taught about complementary colours, opposites on a simple colour wheel, or the difference between hue and tone.

Hue is the name we give to the quality which defines the colour we are using. For example, the difference between, say, red and blue; or we could say that turquoise is a blue with a hue that tends towards green. Tone is lightness or darkness; a colour can tend towards white or black.

You may wish to introduce children the concepts of colour contrasts, colour harmonies, colour intensity (saturation). Children could experiment with colours that are warm or cold, neutral or with colour combinations that are discordant. Commercial printers use a different set of primary colours. Older children will enjoy finding out about how commercial printing works.

The danger in imposing too theoretical an approach is that children will lose some of the spontaneity and enjoyment of simply mixing colours and making discoveries for themselves. It is certainly true that beautiful paintings can be made by children who have never seen a colour wheel and do not know what a complementary colour is. Some artists and teachers would argue that children will make better paintings if they are not introduced to the theory too soon. Discovering and experimenting with colours is key, whether or not colour theory is formally introduced.

You will need: all the equipment needed for colour-mixing (ready-mix paint; containers for different colours; mixing palettes; water in containers; different-sized brushes; rags or sponges), colours from magazines and scrap paper to make colour collections; a colour wheel; information about colour theory if you would like to introduce this to the class.

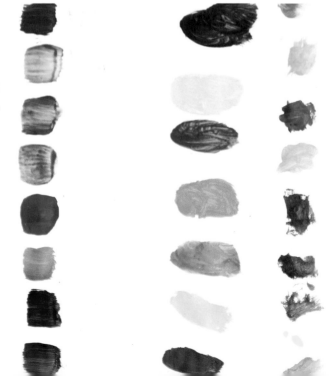

Top : these children had not used acrylic paint before. They are beginning to explore mixing colours. In this case, the class used disposable plates as mixing palettes

Right: colour experiments in acrylic

Starting with tone

Give the children different drawing media. For example, charcoal and chalk, a range of graded pencils, black wax crayons, graphite and felt tip pens. Ask them to experiment in their sketchbooks, or for a more dramatic effect, on larger sheets of paper.

Try and make the darkest patches of tone that you can and then patches that are the lightest or palest possible. Try and make a range of tones that vary from light to dark. Remember you are experimenting, trying to find out how these different drawing media can be used to make light, dark and medium tones. There is no need to draw pictures.

This approach mirrors that used on page 55. The children could also experiment with black and white paint or greens which vary from almost black to nearly white. Now when you take the class outside to look at the landscape you intend to draw or paint, talk about light and dark. Where can children see highlights and shadows? It can also be useful to link work in tone with the topic 'light' in science.

Where can you see the darkest tones in this landscape? Where are the deepest shadows? Can you see any areas that are really light? Can you see any sunlight? If you half close your eyes you can see less detail, but the differences between light and dark tones stand out.

You will need: sketchbooks, or drawing boards and sheets of paper; off-white or buff sugar paper is good for tonal work; a range of drawing media, including differently-graded drawing pencils; the equipment needed for colour mixing, if you would like to explore tone in paint (see facing page).

Starting with space

Talk with the children about what they can see in the foreground, middle-ground and background. You could ask them to make lists. Explain how things look smaller as they get further away. Ask them to comment on examples in the landscape where trees, houses and so forth look tiny in the distance.

Here are three strips of paper. On the first strip, draw everything that you can see way in the distance. Think about the horizon line. On the second strip, draw all the things that are close to us, all the things in the foreground. On the third piece of paper, draw a strip of the middle-ground showing some of the things that are midway between where we are now and the horizon. These are practice drawings so don't worry about making mistakes and drawing too accurately, but try and show as much of the foreground, middle-ground and background as you can.

You will need: sketchbooks or paper and drawing boards; drawing media; strips of paper.

Above: using strips of paper to record only the foreground and background before making a landscape drawing

Starting with line

Ask each of the children to contribute a line of their own to a large sheet of paper. Discuss words or phrases that might be used to describe these lines. Encourage the children to think up new and unusual ways of drawing lines.

Now use your sketchbooks to collect some examples of different lines that you can find by searching around the classroom. There is no need to draw all of the objects you are looking at – just the lines you think are interesting.

I am always amazed by the inquisitiveness of children who will find lines in the most unusual places. This may lead to very inventive drawings.

Now look at the landscape and collect some of the lines you can see. Look out for the horizon line, lines of hedges, roof lines, roads and paths, telephone lines, lines made by trees or clouds. Remember not to draw a picture, just collect lines.

Another good way of investigating line and other visual qualities is by looking at drawings by artists and analysing how the artist has used them. Discuss how the different types of line, shape, texture and tone work.

You will need: sketchbooks or drawing boards and paper; drawing media; a large sheet of paper on an easel for the initial class line collection.

Starting with pattern or texture

Use the same approach, but substitute line for pattern. Work on texture and landscape should be preceded by explorations of mark-making (see page 15).

If you could touch the treetops how do you think they would feel? What would the sky feel like if you could touch it? How about the clouds? Imagine you could reach out and feel the mountainside. What would that be like? Experiment by trying to invent some marks that show how parts of the landscape might feel if you could reach out and touch them. Remember not to draw a picture. You can use some of the ideas you discover to help you make your own landscape picture later.

An aim of this approach is to encourage children to use a variety of marks when they draw. They will then be able to find their own way of representing a mass of leaves, or the faint wispy nature of high cloud.

Drawing the texture of cloud is a difficult concept to grasp. A better approach might be to focus on the marks that artists use to represent clouds or trees. Children could look at a selection of relevant paintings and drawings and mimic the way different artists have used marks to show tactile qualities.

You will need: sketchbooks, or drawing boards and paper; drawing media.

Using these starting points

The starting points for landscape drawing mentioned here focus on the visual qualities. For younger children, or children who have not had much experience of art, it is usually demanding enough to concentrate on one of these qualities at a time. For older or more able children you could combine the tasks above into more complicated exercises. Try shapes that have tones, or colours that have shape and tone, or space shown only by using outline shapes. The variations are endless. The visual qualities are a device that helps us break down visual perception. In reality, these visual qualities work together and it isn't possible to divide them into a single quality. As children become more familiar with the mechanics of rendering colour, tone, shape and so on, it will become more and more natural for them to combine these elements in their work. This experimental and investigative work is also a useful tool for developing descriptive language, as it opens the children's eyes to the visual world that surrounds them. Some would argue that to link talking about the visual environment with corresponding experimental and investigative work in art is the key to creating visually literate children. This literacy benefits both art and language. Even if children are very experienced young artists, it is still worthwhile thinking up a preparatory activity to revise work on a visual quality, or simply to warm the children up to the new task.

Talking about the experiments

Before children begin to paint or draw the landscape, talk about the experimental work. Use these discussions to help suggest possible approaches to painting or drawing the landscape. Some advice about what to say to children before they begin work is detailed in the next session. If you were using the examples above, you would be asking the children to focus on one visual quality. You can adapt this way of working to any subject. Substitute your own topic for landscape and design into a unit of work based upon the ideas described in this chapter.

Above: detail from a child's landscape drawing showing a focus on line and texture. You can see the start of this drawing on page 47

Session 2

Some advice for the children as they make their landscape drawing

The text that follows assumes the children have been exploring shape and tone as starting points. The teacher has found a viewpoint from which the children can draw a landscape. Drawing boards are an essential item of equipment, if children are going to be comfortable when they are drawing (see page 127 for advice on making drawing boards). Use masking tape to hold down the corners of the paper especially on windy days.

Look carefully at the landscape. What can you see that has shape? Where are the most noticeable shapes? Where are the darkest tones? Where are the deepest shadows? Where are there light tones? Can you see light? Remember to concentrate on showing shapes and tones when you draw.

Find the viewpoint you want to draw from. In which direction are you going to look? What is in the centre of the view you are looking at? What are you going to put in the centre of your drawing?

Find the centre of your paper. Start the drawing there. First, draw in an outline shape and then add in a few others around it.

Think about the size of your drawing and the size of your paper. How much of this view do you want to fit into your drawing? How big should your first shapes be?

Draw lightly to start with, and when you think the size and position of your first few shapes is working well, you can press harder to make stronger lines.

Work slowly towards the edges of the paper, adding more shapes as you go.

After a while go back to the centre and start adding in extra details.

Start looking for the very dark tones, the deepest shadows, and begin adding those into the drawing.

Can you draw in some of the medium tones, just like the ones you made when you were experimenting?

Above: outside in the landscape, children can choose a point of view. This location is semi-urban, in a trading estate not far from the school. Many urban parks will offer excellent opportunities for landscape drawing. Notice how essential the drawing boards are to this activity

Right: quiet concentration is important – drawing in this way can lead to absorption. Children will comment that they lose track of time

Try giving children drawing media to work with that they cannot rub out, such as handwriting pens, black wax crayons, black marker pens and biros. Charcoal and chalk on off-white or buff paper would be suitable for drawings with a lot of tonal contrast.

Older children may complain about not being able to rub out their mistakes, but after a while, this strategy should create much more confident and fluent drawings. If you want children to use pencils, you could ban the use of rubbers. Children who are drawing confidently will use rubbers with discretion, so a ban could be a temporary measure. The danger of allowing unlimited use of rubbers right from the start is that some children are so worried about how their drawings are going to look that they never really do any drawing at all. Their paper is just a mass of rubbings out. Making alterations, subtle rearrangements and adjustments, is a vital part of drawing. However, it is much more important first to build children's confidence to draw, to have a go. See page 62 for more advice about helping children with their fear of 'making mistakes'.

If you are using charcoal and chalk on mid-toned paper, ask children to be careful about resting hands and arms on their drawings to avoid unwanted smudging.

Remind them how useful chalk is for showing light. If you are not using charcoal and chalk it is useful to point out that children can leave the paper white if they need to show very light or very bright areas.

Children who bring you their drawings to comment on can be encouraged to look for more shapes or add in more tones. But there is a point at which children are just overwhelmed by too much looking. Many drawings work well without too much detail.

Are you sure you have completely finished? Are there other shapes or tones you can add? Have you included all the important parts of the landscape? Is there a part of your landscape drawing that you can improve? Step back and take a moment to look at your drawing before you decide what to do next, or if you are finished.

Adapt this advice for any of the visual qualities that you may have used as starting points.

You will need: drawing boards and masking tape to hold the paper in place outside; appropriate drawing media, see advice above; hair spray to fix charcoal and chalk.

Top left and top right: children's individual styles as artists quickly become apparent. There is no right way to draw. Each of the two children as well as the boy on page 44 has chosen a very different viewpoint and approach to the drawing

Right: have an informal exhibition in the classroom and talk about the drawings and the activity outside

Session 3

Preparing to make a landscape painting

Children could be working outside or working from drawings they have already made outside and they could also work from photographs they have taken. Paintings made by simply copying a photograph can be very dull and lifeless. Discuss with the children the experience of being in a landscape compared with that of looking at a photograph.

Here is a photograph of the landscape we are going to be painting. What are the main differences between the photograph and the real place? What can the photograph not show about what it is like to be in the landscape itself?

Give children paper to use for testing out colours. Remind them about using the mixing palette, washing and wiping the brush to keep the colours looking clean. Here is a reminder:

Never put a dirty brush into the colour palette. You must always keep the colours you start with clean.

Always wash and wipe the brush.

Mix your colours on the mixing palette before painting on the paper.

Only change the water when it is really dirty, when it looks like cold tea! You only need to wash your mixing palette if there is really no room for a brand new colour. Don't forget that you can mix wonderful new colours by changing colours you have already made. Try adding fresh colour on top of some of the old colours in your mixing palette.

The quality of the painting will be in direct relation to the quality of the preparatory experimental work. It is assumed that the advice that follows will be given to children who have been exploring colour and shape in the landscape.

You will need: all the equipment needed for colour mixing using paint; (see also page 42).

Above: drawing out the composition for a painting using a very pale colour (in this case white). The children know that they will be painting over these lines, which are really guidelines. This helps them to avoid using paint to colour in pencil drawings, which can be tricky. They are beginning to mix colours. They are working from drawings but also have some of the photographs they took at the same time

Right: these girls decided to paint using the kinds of marks they made in their drawings

Right: this is a bolder approach. The artist has decided to explore warm colours he saw in the reed beds. This is not realistic and he may go on to over-paint this again. It is sometimes tempting for an adult to intervene, some would say interfere, if a child is working in an unexpected way. However, it may not be inappropriate and simply reflect creative thinking on the child's part. After all, away from the landscape and back inside, the painting is beginning to dictate its own terms!

Below: there are a wide range of personal styles within one class. Here the child had noted how she achieved certain colour mixes in the experiments which launched this painting activity

Some advice for children as they make their landscape painting

We have talked about colour in the landscape, particularly differences between all the different greens. Try to show that there are lots of different greens in your painting. If you need to, use the scrap of paper to test out your colours first.

You have a thick and a thin brush, use the thick brush for large areas of colour and the thin brush for detail.

To start the painting, mix a very pale colour in the mixing palette and use the thin brush to paint in some outlines of the largest shapes. Only paint a few of these, there is no need to put in lots of detail. This is like drawing although you are using a paintbrush rather than a pencil. The idea is that you can plan what is going into the painting before you start. This means you need to think a little bit about where all the parts of the landscape are going to go on the paper. This is called 'composition'.

The great thing about painting is that it is easy to make changes if you make a mistake, or if you don't like a colour. Just mix some thicker paint and paint over the bits you don't like. You may need to wait a little if the paint you are painting over is still very wet.

Many artists paint large patches of colour first and then gradually add more colour on top. They put detail in at the end. Other artists try to paint all parts of the painting quickly, in one go. They do not paint a background first. Every artist has a personal way of painting. There are many different techniques and styles of painting. Try and find a way to paint that suits you.

Extending children's painting experience

For more experienced children there are many different exercises that you could use to extend their experience of painting.

Children could experiment mixing and using thick and thin paint. They could experiment making different kinds of mark with the brush. These exercises could be linked to work on texture and work on line or mark.

Extend children's awareness of colour with experimental and investigative work using complementary colours, warm and cold colours, bright and dull colours, or concentrate on different colour families such as blues or the tertiary colours, the browns. Look back at page 42.

Importantly, much of children's experience of drawing can be translated into painting; work on shape, space and line can also be important starting points for making landscape paintings.

Some teachers advocate using different kinds of paint such as water colours, poster paints, and even oil paints. Most of the basic exercises and starting points are just as valid whatever the media; and comparisons between how the different media behave can be illuminating. Some of these paints could be of high quality; but they can be very expensive. Children could also experiment using different papers or cards for their paintings.

You will need: all the equipment needed for painting, (see page 42); different kinds of paints; different kinds of brushes; material to add to the paint to make it thicker, PVA for example; different kinds of paper and card.

Above: the painting is nearing completion. It is always worth reminding (without insisting) that children can over-paint parts of a painting several times

Other ideas for work linked to landscape

Stories that are read or made up by children can prompt work on imaginary or fantasy landscapes. There are many paintings by adult artists that will also inspire children to think of unusual ideas. All the preliminary experiments and investigations are just as valid for imaginary landscapes as those based on the real world. Ask children to work on a range of different ideas in rough before deciding on an approach for the painting itself.

Landscape colour can be used as a stimulus for weaving or fabric design. Very tactile woven objects can be made by using materials from the landscape itself, for example, creepers, grass, twigs, reeds, wool, etc. Children could select the colours of different wools, threads or ribbons to give their weaving a similar feel to the landscape they have observed. In this case, considering landscape colour is very much part of a design process.

Patterns for fabrics could be generated from research into landscape shape and colour (see Chapter 2). Children could make relief prints inspired by landscape (see pages 110–111) or adapt drawings to make prints with polystyrene tiles. Different media and techniques could be used to create different effects on the sugar paper which can then used for collage work (see pages 35–39).

Session 4

Talking about landscape paintings or drawings by adult artists, thinking about visual qualities

Many of the ideas about starting points for this project (pages 40–45) can be used to help structure a discussion of the painting or drawing technique used by an adult artist. To summarise, here are some of the points that you could ask the children to comment on:

• Differences between colours from the same family, such as blues, browns or greens

• Warm and cool colours; bright and dull colours; light and dark colours

• The thickness or thinness of the paint used

• The marks and lines the artist has used

• The textures on the surface of the painting and textures of objects represented in paintings

• The shapes

• The space of the painting, including points about foreground, middle-ground and background

• Light and dark parts of the painting; the light in the painting; shadows; questions about where the light is coming from

• Patterns in the painting

Many projects could start by talking about a painting or drawing. Some teachers prefer to leave this discussion to the end of a related activity or even to the end of the whole project, so that the solutions appropriate to adult artists do not influence the children too much.

Above: talking about how artists have made marks with the paint and how they have used colour will give children lots of ideas about how to set about their own painting

Practical exercises that start by talking about a painting

It is possible to launch practical work with visual qualities, by talking about a painting first. Look back at the starting points in this chapter (pages 40–45) and link the activities to a landscape painting. Here are some examples. Children could go on to collect some of the colours and shapes they can see in the painting under discussion. Children could also show the different lines the artist has used or find a way to record the different tonal values of the painting. They could make their own drawing on a strip of paper of the all that they can see in the distance, middle-ground or foreground as they look into a landscape painting. Mark-making experiments could be linked to discussions about textures and the kinds of marks the artist made with the brush.

Talking about landscape paintings focusing on content rather than technique

The approach described above concentrates on some of the formal aspects of a painting or drawing; in other words, how the painting works visually. Knowing about how artists made paintings look the way they do, by using tone, shape, colour and so on, helps children understand how they can manipulate the same qualities in their own work. This way of understanding paintings and drawings will help children develop visual literacy. They will then become more comfortable using this visual language of art, craft and design.

However, it is difficult to separate how paintings and drawings look from their content and meaning. For example, landscape paintings can give children ideas about history (how the landscape might have changed); geography (rivers and mountains for example); biology (a wealth of flora and fauna). Landscape paintings may

be imaginary and inspire links to storytelling and fantasy. In other words it is important to discuss what the paintings show and the feelings generated by the work. It is important to discuss what the art expresses. Some of the most significant landscape paintings in art generate powerful emotions for anyone taking time to look and become absorbed in the painting, even for a short while. All paintings, even abstract ones, show us ideas. With children in the classroom, teachers can help to illuminate some of the ideas and emotions visible in a painting by asking questions:

What can you see when you look at the painting? Make a list of everything that comes to mind. Don't forget to mention the most obvious things as well.

If you could take a walk through the painting what would you pass? What would you see?

What would it be like if you were standing in the painting? What is going on around you?

What is the weather like?

What mood does the painting make you think of? How would you feel if you were actually there?

Does the painting remind you of anywhere or anything?

What do you like about the painting? What do you dislike?

Would you take the painting home and hang it up so you could see it every day? Think of a reason for your answer.

Can you summarise what you think about the painting?

Top: adding the finishing touches to a landscape painting

Opposite: this painting is a result of the same landscape project. This child decided to draw a tiny flower in the grass. This powerful work would not have appeared if the teacher had insisted on a landscape view as the subject

Other strategies for working with paintings and drawings

A rich language exercise can be planned by making comparisons between two or more landscapes. Try looking at approaches to landscape in the work of artists from other cultures. For example, aboriginal Australians use pattern in work that is linked to their environment. In the last thirty years many British artists such as Richard Long, Andy Goldsworthy and David Nash have been creating new forms of landscape-inspired art, much of which relies heavily on pattern-making or the raw qualities of the actual material of the physical landscape. Try using the other visual qualities to make appropriate visual links between different examples of art, craft and design.

Finally, here is a familiar and fun idea for a lesson that might be used to help children investigate a painting:

- A print of a painting was mounted on card. Don't show the children the whole painting!

- A grid of squares or rectangles is then drawn over the print and cut out. The number of squares or rectangles depends on the number of children or groups taking part in the exercise.

- Each child has one cut-out piece of the painting and is asked to try to mix the colours visible in their section of the painting. In other words they have to copy their section on a new square or rectangle.

- When all the pieces of the painting have been copied by the group or class, it is reassembled and compared with the original.

- The project works best if the children do not know in advance what the completed painting looks like. Different children will approach the task in different ways. Children will clearly see that each individual has a style of painting of their own.

5

Portraits

Session 1

Starting points and collecting shapes from a head

Starter activities are equally valid for this portrait project as they were in the previous chapter about landscape. So, it is worthwhile taking another look at landscape drawing and painting (see pages 40–45).

The first session is designed to help children focus on the shapes they can see in a head, prior to drawing a portrait. Begin this work by reminding children about the concept of shape (see pages 76 and 77).

Ask children to use their sketchbooks or drawing boards and paper and collect some of the individual features (eyes, mouth, nose, etc.) that make up the head.

Look carefully at the shape of the nose, look at the nose from the side and from the front. Draw the nose shape from at least two different angles. You could try looking down on a nose from above or up at a nose from below! Concentrate on the outline shape. Collect some other examples of nose shapes. Look at eyes, mouths, ears, hair styles in the same way. Make sure you have several examples of each. Remember not to draw the whole portrait, just collect the shapes of the various features.

Starting with tone

Ask children to make some tonal experiments. (See page 43.) For example, if you are going to use pencils for the portrait drawing, first give the children a selection of different grades of drawing pencil, say 4B, 2B, HB and H. Ask them to experiment creating a series of tonal patches. Ask the children to comment on the relative qualities of the different pencils. This activity could be adapted for any combination of drawing media.

Which of the media you used made the darkest tones? Which one made the faintest marks? Which pencil shows up the clearest?

You will need: sketchbooks, or drawing boards and paper; graded drawing pencils or other drawing media.

Collecting tones from a head

Look carefully at your partner's head. Where can you see the darkest tones? Are there any parts of the head that are black? Where can you see shadows? Where are the deepest shadows? Are there any areas of skin that are darker than others? Does all the hair have the same tone?

Collect some of the shadows and dark parts of the head. For example, just draw the shadows around the nose or under the mouth or around the ears. See if you can draw a nose or an eye or a mouth by using patches of different tones.

Practice drawing a small patch of skin or hair. Use the pencil to show how there are a number of different

tones even in quite a small area of skin or hair. Just as before, don't draw the whole head. You are practising drawing tones.

The children's drawings may not look like anything very much, but they are focusing on tone and practising using appropriate drawing media. If you are able to help children see the value of exploring and experimenting, even if the end products don't at first appear to be finished images, they will progress far faster in art. They will also progress in their capacity to think creatively and take creative risks in their work.

You will need: sketchbooks, or drawing boards and paper; graded drawing pencils or other drawing media.

Starting with texture

Mirror the approach used above but, this time, focus on the textural qualities of a head. For example, ask the children to use drawing pencils to try and show the difference between skin and hair. Encourage the children to experiment with different ways of using a pencil until they have found a method that works well.

You could also look at clothing in this way. For example, ask the children to explore ways of recording the differences in texture between wool and polyester or cotton.

You will need: sketchbooks, or drawing boards and paper; graded drawing pencils or other drawing media.

Left: exploring different possibilities for parts of a head. This sheet is a warm-up activity before drawing an imaginary portrait. Notice that the child is experimenting with both a soft drawing pencil and charcoal

Above: children can experiment with a range of media to create tone

Starting with colour

Look at the back of your hand. What colours can you see? Use pastels or paint to try and mix some skin colours. Make a collection of colours in your sketchbook. Is there another way you could collect skin colours? Try cutting out different examples of skin colours from colour magazines. Glue fragments of skin colour into your sketchbooks.

The children could go on to match some of the colours collected from magazines by mixing with pastels or paint. Ask each child to cut a large colour photograph of a head and shoulders in half, lengthways. Use a photograph from a colour magazine. Glue one half onto paper. Ask the children to complete the missing half in paint or pastels. How close can they come to matching the colours from the photograph?

You will need: sketchbooks, or paper and drawing boards; photographs from magazines; scissors; glue; all the equipment needed for mixing colours in pastels (sugar paper; pastels); all the equipment needed for mixing colours in paint (ready-mix paint; containers for different colours; mixing palettes; water in containers; different-sized brushes; rags or sponges).

Above: taking it in turns to be the artist and the model. Children can swap every five minutes or so

Below: it's always difficult to capture skin tones but children will enjoy the challenge

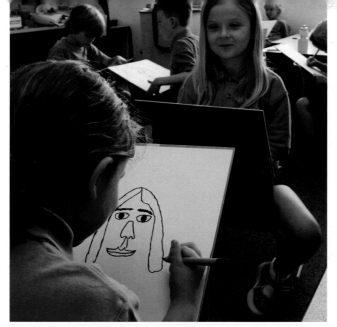

Session 2

Drawing the head and shoulders

Ask each child to find a partner. Each pair should have one drawing board and one set of drawing media between them. Children will take it in turns to be a model and an artist.

Look carefully at the head of the model. What shape would you start with? Choose a shape from the middle of the head. The nose is a good place to start. Draw the shape of the nose just above the middle of your paper.

Look for some more shapes. How about the shapes that make up the eyes? Draw those in next. Keep looking and drawing until you have drawn the most important shapes from the head.

Look at the shapes of the clothing that the model is wearing. Look at the collar and the neck. Are there any patterns in the clothes you can see?

Look carefully at the shape of the chin, hair and eyebrows. Look carefully at the shape of the whole head. It is not an exact circle or oval. Try and draw the shape that you see.

Now look for shadows. Start by drawing in the very darkest tones. Then add in more shadows and tones from each part of the head.

This method is concentrating on shape and tone. You could use colour and texture as a focus, or tone and colour; or shape and texture. Try asking older and more advanced children to work thinking about three or four basic elements, say, shape, tone, colour and texture.

You will need: sketchbooks, or drawing boards and paper; graded drawing pencils or other drawing media – for example, pastels if you decide to work in colour.

Some advice for children drawing a portrait

You will need to think big, Try to imagine the size of the head and shoulders on the paper. How big should the nose be? Start slowly and draw the first nose shape lightly. You can always make it bigger if it is too small to start with.

Look at the position of the eyes. If your partner is looking straight at you, the eyes will be halfway between the top of the head and the chin. Look for the position of the mouth. Look at where the hairline goes. Where are the tops and bottoms of the ears?

Even very experienced artists find drawing portraits difficult. You are bound to make mistakes. Sometimes your portrait might look strange. Don't worry; the more you practice the easier it will be to make a better drawing next time.

If you want your portrait to look like the model, pick something that really stands out about the person you are drawing. Is the hair style distinctive? Are the clothes noticeable? Is your partner wearing jewellery or anything in their hair? Concentrate hard on making your drawing look distinctive.

Top left: drawing boards make it possible for children to adapt the classroom into a drawing studio. This girl is drawing with a thin felt-tip pen. This makes strong, clear marks and she can't rub out mistakes. When children first start drawing, this really helps build confidence

Top right: a detail of a finished observational portrait

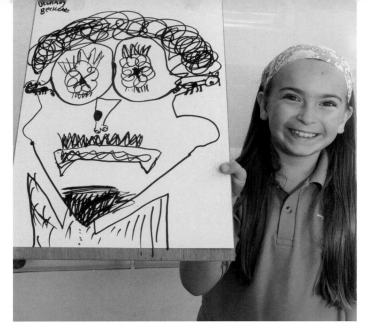

Challenge older and more advanced children by asking them to observe two or three children looking in different directions. One child could look straight ahead, another to the side and a third could be looking up or down. They will have to think carefully about the features and where they are in relation to each other. For example, if the head is tilted back, the eyes may appear near the top of the outlined head in the drawings.

Imaginative portraits

It is always valuable to offer children opportunities to engage their imagination, particularly as a counterweight to observing and recording in a realistic way. Look at the photographs on this page. These imaginative portraits were made after warming-up by exploring and experimenting with shape. Children collected and invented shapes of parts of a head such as eyes, mouths, noses and hair. Following some of the general advice on drawing heads and shoulders, as well as how to draw with confidence (see page 62), they then went on to create imaginative portraits. This project could also be a catalyst for drama, as well as expressive and descriptive writing, as children will be highly motivated to talk and write about the characters they have created.

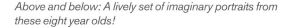

Above and below: A lively set of imaginary portraits from these eight year olds!

Left: this class talked about British artist Frank Auerbach's portrait drawings. They decided that his hand would skip across the paper and always be restless before making their own portrait drawing in the style of Auerbach

Below left: Head of Catherine Lampert *1986 by Frank Auerbach, oil on canvas*

Below right: Head of Julia *1989 by Frank Auerbach, charcoal and chalk*

Session 3

Looking at portraits and drawing a portrait inspired by the style of an artist

Pick a selection of portraits by adult artists to show the children – postcards or printouts are useful for group work. You may need larger prints if you wish to talk about portraits with the whole class. You will find many examples of portraits online, particularly if you visit the online collections of major art galleries and museums. If you are projecting images onto a whiteboard, try to make sure that children can really see the images clearly. All too often, poor blackout means projected images look washed out and difficult to see. Of course, there is no substitute for visiting an art gallery to look at original portraits.

Ask the children to make a portrait of their partner in the style of one of the portraits they have been talking about. It is important to spend some time discussing the characteristics of the artist's work. The nineteenth-century artist Auguste Renoir used technique and colour in a very different way from Francis Bacon who was working at the end of the last century. One artist can also use different approaches throughout a lifetime; Picasso's cubist portraits are very different from those made earlier or later in his life. Artists from different cultures approach portraiture in very different ways. It is helpful to compare different approaches, so that children can make an informed choice about the 'style' they would like to adopt for their own work.

Let's make a list together of everything you can see in the portrait.

Now we can talk about some of the visual qualities. Where can you see different tones? Where are there shadows or highlights? Can you see different textures? What about the colours the artist has used?

What sort of person is shown in the portrait? What character do you think they have? How are they

feeling? How has the artist given the person in the portrait a character? How would you describe their expression? Is there anything in the background or around them that can help us understand more about them?

Which is the best painting we have talked about? Which would you choose to put up on a wall at home? What are the reasons for your choice? Do you think a friend would choose a different painting?

As a practical starter, you could give children a viewfinder. This is a small window cut into a sheet of paper or card. Children can use the viewfinder to isolate certain areas of the portrait. They can then collect various qualities or features, for example: different facial expressions, tones or textures, or they could mix colours they can see through the 'window' of the viewfinder. There is a photograph on page 23 of a child using a viewfinder as part of another project.

When they go on to make their own portrait 'in the style of', they do not need to mimic everything about the style of a chosen artist. Ask the children to pick one or two characteristics of their favourite portrait to use in their own drawing. They could choose the background or the style of clothing. Perhaps they could try to use the colour scheme or even make similar lines and marks to the ones the artist used. Oil pastels are a good medium to use for this activity. They have a richness of colour and allow for different methods of application.

You will need: sketchbooks, or drawing boards and paper; drawing media; a selection of portraits by adult artists: Rembrandt, Van Gogh and artists from Renaissance Italy are popular examples from our culture; search out some portraits by contemporary artists; extend the project by looking at portraits and heads drawn by artists from different cultures.

Right and opposite: finished observational and imaginative portrait drawings

Painting a portrait

The class can go on to paint a portrait. Ask the children to follow some of the steps outlined in this chapter but using paint, rather than drawing media. A key to working in paint is to think of it as a natural extension of drawing. Make sure that the children learn to draw in paint with a brush, rather than drawing in pencil first and then filling colours with paint. Ask them to start their portrait by mixing a very pale colour in the mixing palette. They can draw some of the important shapes in their portrait with a thin brush, using this pale colour. Encourage the children to paint over mistakes. Once children are happy to paint one colour over another, their painting will quickly become more fluent. Much of the advice appropriate to painting landscapes could be repeated here, so look back at page 49.

You will need: all the equipment needed for painting (see page 42).

6

Figure drawing

Session 1

Building confidence

Confidence about drawing is always an issue when drawing figures. It is natural for both children and teachers to want their drawings to look real, like real people. Naturally, children in primary school are inexperienced artists and so as yet, most do not have the skills or the experience to draw with conventional realism. It is important that they understand that they are still learning about drawing and, just as with all new and difficult tasks, they need practice. Skill is a quality that develops slowly, backed up by a great deal of practice. Specialist education in music or sport encourages a culture of practice that is sometimes very repetitious. Children often find it boring even if adults emphasise its necessity. In the last fifty years, art education specialists have increasingly looked upon repetition and technical practice for its own sake with suspicion, as they argue that the first aim of art education should be to promote original and meaningful creativity. Whether or not too much restriction and prescription will do harm, and no matter what our views are about the relative merits of purely technical exercises, there is no doubt that the limited time available for art in school is best used to give children a broad base of experience. This means that children will not often have the opportunity to practice drawing figures. Teachers should help them to understand that they will find it very hard to draw figures accurately or realistically to begin with. But it can be rewarding to try, and paying attention to the visual qualities will help children find an angle, a focus, that will improve their drawings. As children grow older and have more opportunities to draw, they will find that just as in all their work, they will improve and grow in confidence with practice.

The emphasis on 'shape' in landscape, portrait and figure work is deliberate. This simple-to-understand quality can be used as an underlying foundation to help children draw many of the familiar subjects they will come across in school. Children will soon recognise that concentrating on shape can underpin their drawing. It will become natural and normal for children to look for shapes when they draw. The other visual qualities (line, pattern, colour, form, space, tone and texture) can interlink with and develop in parallel with the confidence gained from children's increasingly articulate drawing of shape.

Looking for the outline shapes of figures

Use one of the warm-up exercises to help children refocus on shape. Even if children are experienced artists it is still helpful to find a way to revise this concept. (Look at pages 76 and 77 for more ideas.) You might begin this project by drawing around body shapes with chalk in the playground. This will help to reinforce the concept of shape in relation to the outlines of figures. The children will see the huge variety of shapes a figure can make. Time spent looking and talking will be well rewarded. Use volunteers to demonstrate the many different kinds of shapes the body can make.

She has made her body into a shape that reminds me of a bridge. Can anyone else think of a different shape that they could make with their bodies? Come out and show us.

This body shape looks very sad. Someone who looked like this might be very unhappy. Can you think of any other emotions that we can show with our bodies? Try happy, excited, tired and shy – now for some ideas of your own!

The children can act out these shapes in groups, or work out a number of ideas on their own. Children can take photographs to record the various shapes they make with their bodies. This can become part of a wider project. For example, see page 120 in the section that describes an issue-led project with the theme of conflict and fear.

You will need: chalk to draw around children lying in the playground; a camera to photograph some of their body shapes.

Drawing the body shapes

Ask for volunteers to pose in one of the shapes the children discovered. Children can now draw outlines of a figure in their sketchbooks or on paper mounted on drawing boards. Ask them not to add too much detail. There is no need to draw eyes, noses, mouths and so on. It is the outline that is important. Remind them not to worry about mistakes. It is important that all the class or group can see the model. Improvise a table as a stage, or use a large open space for this work, such as the hall or the playground. Extra adult supervision is necessary. Children should make a number of different drawings on one piece of paper. They are making a collection of outline shapes of figures from different viewpoints. If they have printouts of the photographs they took, these can be added to the collection.

Draw the outline shape of the model on your paper. Allow space for about four drawings. When everyone has finished their first drawing, we will change the viewpoint you have by asking the model to make the same pose but facing a different way. You only need draw what you can see. Do not draw anything you cannot see. If you have a back view or a side view, draw that. You will have four different drawings of the same pose.

This can be hard work for the model! It is also possible for the model to stay in the same pose and for children to move to different positions for each drawing. This exercise is also relevant to developing an understanding of space in drawing in relation to the viewpoint of the artist.

Above: collecting outline shapes of figures in various poses

Right and below: the classroom becomes an art school for this activity. Children move position to capture the figures from different points of view

Talking about figure drawings

Artists from many different eras and cultures have drawn the human figure. It is not difficult to find examples to show children. The Italian Renaissance artists produced many figure drawings. Some of the best examples to use are from artists' sketchbooks. Look for figure drawings by Leonardo, Michelangelo and Raphael. You could research figure drawings by contemporary artists. Some of these drawings were often made very quickly. The children can see that even famous artists make 'mistakes'. For example, some artists may draw a line to show the shoulder a number of times in the same drawing. Drawings sometimes resemble experiments or try-outs as the artist searches for what he or she is looking for.

You will need: sketchbooks, or drawing boards and paper; drawing media; reproductions of figure drawings.

Session 2

Using stockinette to simplify the shape and form

Remind the children about tone – light and dark. The visual quality of tone and the effects of light and shade are going to be essential for the drawings. Try a simple warm-up exercise (see page 55). If children are using charcoal and chalk, the mixing needed in this exercise can be subtle, so even if they are very experienced with this media it well worth setting some time aside for practising delicate mixes of black and white before starting the central activity.

The way we use the words 'shape' and 'form' is confusing in the English language. Adults as well as children find it difficult to work out what is meant by the word 'form'. The form of a figure is the shape it takes in three dimensions. However, as we have seen, figures drawn on paper have a two-dimensional shape although it is possible for two-dimensional drawings to show form. To help clarify this for children, you could reserve the word 'form' for talking about objects in three dimensions, and use the word 'shape' when you mean a shape in two dimensions.

The following sequence of activities builds on what has gone before. You will need a stockinette, which is available online. Use the following exercise to introduce older children to the relationship between shape and form. Ask for a volunteer to try on the stockinette. It is an elasticised tube of knitted fabric available in rolls that will slip over the head and can be dragged down to the feet. It is better if the whole body is hidden by the net. Tie a knot in the top and then tuck the bottom end under the child's feet.

What can you see? How would you describe this body sculpture? What has happened to the body? What can't you see? What does the body remind you of?

Ask the model to try different poses. For example, ask the child inside the tube to push out their hands, or bend in different ways. Ask the other children for more ideas about what the model can do. You will find some interesting effects using different props like furniture or apparatus from the hall. Children can take it in turns to pose. Try posing two or three children together!

The activity could have a definite focus, for example, you could talk about an emotion like sorrow. How can the figure, wrapped in the elastic net, appear sorrowful? You could refer to the figures as body sculptures.

You will need: stockinette and a variety of props; use a camera to record the various poses.

Above: the stockinette simplifies the forms of figures as they become live body sculptures. Children will go on to discover about the sculpture and drawings of Henry Moore

Drawing the body sculptures

Choose a pose to draw. Organise the children to draw as before. These photographs give plenty of clues about one way of organising space in the classroom. This activity ideally needs extra adult supervision. This time, before they draw, remind them about tone. Ask them to look at the figure and decide where the lightest tones are and where the darkest tones are. Talk about shadows and highlights. Remind them about shape. You could choose a paper that is neutral in colour and tone, perhaps light grey or buff sugar paper.

Use charcoal and chalk to draw the body sculpture. Use chalk to draw the shape very lightly at first. If you make a mistake you can easily redraw a new shape over the first one. Use the chalk again to show the light tones. Then use the charcoal to show dark tones. Look for shadows. You will need to be careful about how you use the charcoal with the chalk. Work slowly and think carefully about the greys you need to make. As you add tone, your drawings of the body sculptures will show three-dimensional form.

The children can go on to draw groups of body sculptures. Or perhaps they could work on one large drawing rather than a series of small ones.

Talking about the sculptures and drawings of Henry Moore

Many teachers would introduce these at the start of the project, and this approach can also work well. However, the advantage here is that children are not influenced by Moore's drawings in advance, but come to understand something of his work after their own attempts. Moore was first and foremost a sculptor, and his drawings are often very tonal. He used contrasts between light and dark to represent three-dimensional forms in two dimensions. In this project, shadows and highlights help to show the form of figures, so they look rounded rather than flat. This can be complicated to explain to children, but this project makes the point in a practical way. Older and more experienced children will be especially fascinated. After looking at and talking about the drawings, show the children examples of Moore's sculptures. Talk about the similarities between their drawings of the body sculptures and Moore's work.

You will need: stockinette and a variety of props; charcoal and chalk; grey, buff or off-white sugar paper; drawing boards and masking tape; hairspray or fixative to fix the drawings (use carefully); images of Henry Moore's drawings and sculptures to show children.

Top left: drawing a body sculpture in this class of eight year olds

Top right: notice how this child has investigated ways of showing tonal differences on the left of his drawing. The boy immediately behind has a very different approach and is exaggerating the shadows so that they are black

Opposite: a good example of exploring how to draw tonally in order to show form

7

Figures and heads in clay

Session 1

Learning about clay

Even older children will need to experience some of the simple properties and possibilities of clay if they are new to the media. Here is an example of how a teacher might explain some important points about using clay to the class.

We have protected the tables to keep them clean and make tidying up easier. You also have wooden boards to work on. You can slide and turn the work around by moving the boards. This means that you don't have to keep picking up your sculptures, which is a problem if the clay is soft and the sculptures are delicate. You can easily damage what you have just made.

There are some tools you can use to cut or change the clay in different ways.

Each of you has a lump of clay to work with. The clay is wrapped in a small polythene food bag ready for you to use. Why do you think we need to keep clay wrapped up like that?

There is also a sponge on the table. The sponge is damp, but it is not wringing wet. There shouldn't be any drips even if you squeeze the sponge. As you use the clay it will begin to dry out. If the clay is too dry it will begin to crack and crumble and become difficult to use. You can often tell if this is likely to happen by looking at your hands. If the clay on your hands is turning lighter and feeling dry and dusty, it's probable that the clay you are using is too dry. What do you think would happen if we added water to the clay? The danger is that the clay would become so sticky that not only would it be difficult to make anything good, but everything, including you, would get in a terrible mess! Never just add water to the clay. So, if your hands feel dry, just press them onto the damp sponge and keep on working. That is enough dampness to keep the clay in the right condition to use.

On the table is some slip together with an old paint brush. The slip is a mixture of clay and water. It has the consistency of double cream. You can use the slip like runny glue. If you need to join two pieces of clay together, use the paintbrush and the slip. This helps to make sure your sculptures do not fall apart when they dry. You will also need to press the pieces of clay firmly together. To make an even stronger join, make criss-cross marks in the clay where it will be joined. If you apply the slip onto the criss-cross areas (they are like lots of tiny grooves) and press the clay firmly together, the slip sinks into the grooves and makes a stronger bond.

Left: starting with simple forms quickly leads children to discover ways of making figures

Below: it is always important to give children an opportunity to learn about clay

Look out for little bits of clay that break off. These can fall on the floor or clutter up your working space. Try to collect all the little bits of clay every now and then while you are working. Artists know how important it is to keep their work space organised and tidy. The best way of collecting little bits of clay is to use a small spare lump of clay and dab it onto all the little bits on the table or your board. The bits will stick to the lump.

A simple science experiment to observe changes in clay

Design a simple experiment to help children understand what happens to clay as it dries out over a period of time. Leave some clay out in the classroom and as a comparison, wrap another piece of clay in a sealed polythene bag. Leave more clay outside, or in a cool damp place. Finally, leave clay in different containers, some with lids, some without. Ask children to look out for changes in how the clay feels, its colour and any changes to the containers themselves over several days. A container with a lid on may show condensation as water evaporates out of the clay.

Starting with simple forms

If children are using clay for the first time, or it has been quite a while since it was last used, ask them to experiment by making simple three-dimensional forms such as cuboids, cylinders, spheres, pyramids, etc. When they have a collection of simple forms they can use the slip to join them together to make a sculpture. The children will quickly discover that they can assemble the basic three-dimensional forms into clowns, trains, cars, rockets, robots, aliens and so forth. This is a useful way to introduce using clay and allows children to practise and explore how the material and equipment work.

You will need: basic grey or earthenware clay; store the clay in polythene food bags which can be sealed – this means you can prepare the clay in advance; cheese wire or an old blunt kitchen knife to cut the clay (use carefully with children); slip (a mixture of clay and water at a consistency of double cream); clay tools (these can be purchased but lollypop sticks work quite well); protection for tables (in the photographs, children are working on tables with hardboard covers – hardboard can be cut to the size of the tables you use in class); boards to work on; old paint brushes to apply slip; damp sponges; rags to wipe sticky hands.

Session 2

Making small figures in clay or Plasticine

The drawing activities on page 63 are starting points for this project. Plasticine is an alternative to clay for making small figures, but make sure the Plasticine is malleable before children use it. It performs better when slightly warm, so leave it in a sunny window or near a radiator. With Plasticine, the work could be developed into a stop-frame animation project.

There are two ways the children can explore making figures in clay. It is worth explaining both methods because most children will use a combination of the two.

Method 1:

Here is a ball of clay. It is quite small, so your figures will only be around 10cm high. Try to make the form of a body. Then see if you can squeeze out the arms, legs and a head. Go slowly. Try not to make the legs and arms so thin that they fall off. If your figure is not coming out well just squash the clay into a ball and try again. Don't forget to use the sponge to moisten your hands if the clay gets too dry.

Method 2:

Which of the simple forms do arms and legs remind you of? Yes, long cylinders. Now try modelling the head and body out of one lump of clay and then use more clay to make the arms and legs separately. Use slip to join them to the body.

The children will come across many problems. The legs and arms will be too thin and fall off. They will try to stand their figures up and the legs will just not be strong enough. Warn them in advance about the problems and discuss possible solutions. Or suggest that they have two separate attempts at the activity, the first to find out about the problems, the second to see if they can work out solutions. If you have given children the opportunity to try out both methods of making a small figure, it is likely that they will end up using a combination of the two to make their own mini-figure sculptures.

Now you are getting the hang of making small figures, think about the pose you would like your figure to have. What is your figure doing? What is your figure feeling? Could you work together and use all the figures to make one group? Is there anything else that you could make to go with the figure? Sometimes combining two or more figures or making some props will help support the sculptures.

Warn the children that however careful they have been, the clay figures may crack as they dry. One well known installation called *Field* by British artist Antony Gormley uses thousands of clay figures. The work takes many forms depending on where it is shown and has been exhibited all over the world. Search for images and information via the internet. This may suggest a possible outcome for children's own small clay figures. They might look quite spectacular as a crowd!

You will need: clay, either buff-cloured or eathernware; plastic foodbags to keep the clay moist; wooden boards for children to work on; clay tools.

Above: Field (American) *by Antony Gormley, 1991, Terracotta. Photograph by Joseph Coscia, JR, Courtesy of White Cube*

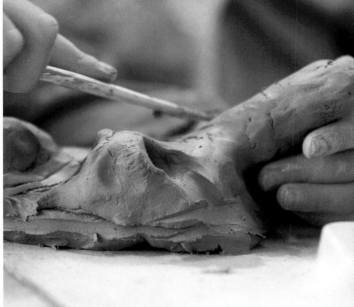

Session 3

Using the stockinette drawings and the sculptures of Henry Moore as a prompt for figure sculptures

Look back to page 66. Start with that work and repeat the preceding session, only this time, ask children to simplify the form of their figures. Their own small figures may be influenced by Henry Moore's sculptures.

Go on to ask the children if they can think of other ways to change the form of their figure sculptures. You could show them the work of sculptors such as Giacometti, Barbara Hepworth as well as Antony Gormley. Introduce them to examples of figure sculptures from other cultures. For example, show pictures of figures from Easter Island. This is an opportunity to explore how clay tools can be used to change the forms.

Children will gain many ideas simply talking about the sculptures you show them and what they are finding out when they use the clay.

You will need: all the equipment needed for using clay (see page 69); images of figure sculpture by artists such as Moore, Hepworth, Giacometti and Gormley; images of figure sculptures from other cultures; the children's own figure drawings (see page 66).

Top left: clay can be hollowed, smoothed, carved and changed in many ways

Top right: learning more about how to use clay tools

Right: looking at Henry Moore's sculptures. These children talked about the formal qualities, such as surface, and how the sculptures are like human figures

Session 4

Making heads in clay

The starting point for this project might be portrait drawing. Or you could begin by showing the children sculptural heads. The children's clay heads could be imagined or based on observation. This project can easily be adapted to a specific theme.

This is a project where it is necessary to demonstrate the process in advance, but it is not difficult to do. This is how you might describe the process to the children. Part of the introduction should focus on the fact that children will be working in the round. They will be considering the head from different angles and viewpoints.

We are going to make a head and shoulders in clay. What will be the differences between a head made out of clay and one drawn on paper? What will be good about making heads in clay instead of drawing?

As well as clay and the usual equipment, we are also going to need newspaper, masking tape and paper bags. This is a piece of cardboard that we can use as a base for the sculpture.

Put three sheets of newspaper together. Cut a long strip about 15 cm wide. Roll the strip into a tube. Use the masking tape to stop the tube unravelling.

At one end of the tube make about four short cuts. Bend the newspaper back to make tabs. Use the masking tape to tape these tabs flat onto the cardboard base, so the tube stands up. This is the support for the neck.

Roll up a sheet of newspaper into a ball. Put it into the paper bag to stop it unravelling. Now tape the open end of the bag around the top of the tube. Use plenty of tape. This is the support for the head.

I have cut some clay from the clay bag using this cheese wire. You can roll this out to make sheets of clay. Not too thick, but not so thin that the clay will split and break. Mould the sheets of clay around the tube to make the neck. Now use more clay to make the shoulders. Do that now to give the neck support. Use more sheets of clay to mould around the paper head. Smooth down the joins as you go. Take care to make sure the head is well joined to the neck.

Check to see if any of the newspaper or bag is showing. If this is happening, cover up the gaps with more clay. Are you happy with the general form of the shoulders, neck and head? Now is the time to make changes. You can be quite rough with the clay because at the moment there are no delicate features to spoil.

Now we can add the features. Think about where the eyes should go. Not too near the top of the head! Use your thumbs to press in the eye sockets. Roll some clay to make the eyeballs. Don't forget to use the slip. Make a nose and use the slip to fix it to the head. Use a clay tool to press in a line for the mouth. Add on lips, ears, eyebrows, nostrils and other features or characteristics.

Look carefully at your clay head. Think about the chin, the forehead, cheekbones. Turn the head around. Are you pleased with the form of the back of the head? Make any changes or additions you think are needed. Has the head got an expression? Can you tell what sort of a character your head has? You may want to change some of the features to give more character or more expression to the sculpture. Now you can add the hair. Use thin strips of clay and the slip. Perhaps you can give you head a hairstyle? Is the hair curly, straight, plaited, or dreadlocked?

Opposite left: first make a strong tube out of paper and fix this to the cardboard base with masking tape

Opposite right: next, a paper bag filled with newspaper can be attached to the tube. This can be quite rough and ready at this stage. Children can use masking tape to wrap around the bag to help give it form

Right: being able to work together is important. These eight-year-old children worked in groups of three. As they get older, children can work more independently if they choose

Below: slivers or sheets of clay can be wrapped around the paper. It's best to start with the neck and shoulders so that the sculpture is supported from the base

As that is a lot of information all in one go, it might be better to make the heads in stages, or at least to give the instructions in stages. If you need to spread this making activity over a number of days, spray the head with a plant mister at the end of each session and cover with a plastic bag, tucking the ends under the base. The clay will be fine as long as it is kept damp.

Another technique that can be used to make larger imaginary creatures or figures is based on the principle of coiling clay. The children do not use a paper support for their work; instead they build the basic structure out of coils of clay held together with slip.

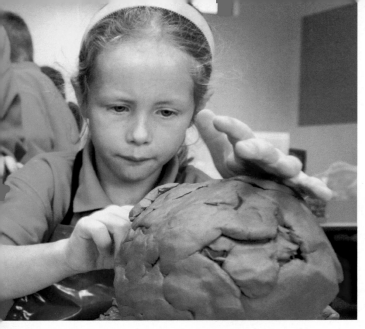

Firing and glazing the heads

It is not possible here to give detailed information about firing and glazing. Seek advice from the art department in your local college, secondary school or high school. Some potters will agree to fire work for a small charge. Firing and glazing clay creates new opportunities to help children understand how different processes affect and change materials that artists use for art and design. This means that the characteristics of a chosen process will be very important when thinking about the way an end product may look.

If the heads are to be fired, gently remove the paper support from inside when the heads are dry. Most of it will pull out. Don't worry too much if some remains inside; it will burn away in the kiln.

Although this is a technical project and the activity is prescribed to some extent, the confidence that teachers and children will get from seeing the heads develop is worth the effort. It may be argued that it is better for children to work in this media in this way than to deny them opportunity for purely technical reasons. The technique may not be perfect, the end products may be flawed in the eyes of an expert, but the value of the experience is undeniable. For this reason, it is fine to leave the heads unfired although they will be delicate. They can be coated with a 50/50 mixture of PVA glue and water (this will act as a kind of varnish) and carefully painted.

You will need: all the equipment needed for using clay (see page 69); rolling pins; newspaper; masking tape; scissors; paper bag; cardboard for a base; PVA glue, brushes and water pots for varnishing (optional).

Top left: using clay tools to sculpt the face

Right: this head was an imaginary character and was a spin-off from imaginative portrait drawings (see page 58)

Top right and opposite: to sculpt a head from clay on this scale is quite an achievement. Children recognised just how much they had learnt and just how much they had enjoyed the process. This is a good example of the opportunities offered by skills and techniques alongside more open creativity

8

Drawing buildings

Session 1

Re-examining the concept of shape

Children should already be familiar with the visual qualities. However, these concepts may need to be re-examined. If children from seven to eleven years old have never been taught this approach to drawing before then it will be necessary to find a way of helping them to focus on shape. This basic investigative and explorative work underpins many of the projects in this book. The work in this session was originally designed for younger children but it can be adapted easily as a starter or warm-up activity for older children.

Talking about shapes

Look around the room. Can you see any shapes? Let's make a list of the shapes you can see. Who can see a shape that is bigger than I am? Who can see a shape that is smaller than your hand?

Children will immediately think of the shapes they have learnt in maths. The first step is to link the shapes they know through maths with the shapes of different objects and images they can see in the room.

Drawing around shapes and finding out about outlines

Look. I can draw a line around this shape. This is an outline. I can find the outline of all sorts of things. What shall I try next? A spoon? A key? Let's try a few more. These outlines make shapes. Look at the shapes we have drawn. We can recognise an object by the shape it has. Now you can try drawing around more things to make shapes of your own.

After you have made a few outline shapes with the children, ask them to collect some more on their own. Provide a collection of interesting objects or the children could hunt around the classroom and discover shapes for themselves. Afterwards, they could try and guess the objects that go with the outlines that other children have collected.

Right: collecting shapes found in the classroom (reproduced from Teaching Art 4–7)

Below: collecting shapes outside

You will need: a large sheet of paper on an easel or drawing board to demonstrate drawing around shapes; paper and drawing boards or sketchbooks to collect outlines; soft pencils, small black wax crayons, felt-tips or handwriting pens for making good, clear outlines.

Finding shapes by looking

The children have been drawing around objects to make shapes. The next sequence of activities should help them collect different outlines by looking and drawing.

I want to collect the shape of the large window in the classroom. What are the problems?

Look. If I close one eye and point at the window, I can trace around the outside of the frame to draw a shape in the air. Let's all practise.

Here is a black wax crayon. I can look at the window and instead of tracing around the frame with my finger in the air, I can draw the shape with the crayon on the paper. This time I am using a crayon, not my finger and I am drawing on the paper, not in the air. I have to look carefully at the shape of the window.

Look at the shape I've drawn. Now you can find the shape of anything you want to. Just look carefully, trace around the shape in the air with your finger, and then draw the outline on the paper. Let's try and draw the shape of this electric fan together. Tell me some of the other things in the room which have outline shapes.

Children could collect shapes of things much bigger than they are, or they could even look out of the window and collect shapes of things outside. The children should look carefully, but they shouldn't worry about making mistakes. The important thing is that they are looking at and drawing shapes. If they make attractive drawings, that is a bonus. Soon they won't need to race the shapes with their fingers; they will just look and draw.

Collecting shapes by looking and drawing

Now you can collect all kinds of different outlines by looking and drawing. See how many you can find. Don't draw too much detail inside your shape. It's the outline that's important.

Talking about the shapes you have collected

Who found an outline shape of something very large or something very small? Who found an outline shape with straight lines or with curves? Who found an outline shape with bumps or points? Did anyone find an unusual shape? How would you describe it?

Session 2

Collecting shapes inside shapes

This is a revision exercise that could follow on from the previous session. Focusing on shapes inside shapes is an important component of the strategy for drawing buildings.

Now I'd like you to find objects or images that have smaller shapes contained inside larger outline shapes. Who can think of some ideas? The computer keyboard is a good example. Now try and collect a few examples in your sketchbooks. Draw in the larger outline shape first, and then put the smaller shapes you can see inside.

Looking for shapes in buildings

You will need to take the children to look at a building or buildings. The school building is an obvious choice but there may be houses, shops, factories and places of worship that can be seen without even leaving the school playground.

When you look at the building, where can you see shapes? What parts of the building have a shape? Are there examples of shapes that have smaller shapes inside them? Are any of the shapes repeated to make patterns?

Collecting building shapes by drawing

Draw some of the shapes you can see when you look at this building. Don't draw all the building. Don't spend too long on any one drawing. It is important to collect a variety of different shapes. Don't forget you can look for and draw shapes inside the main shapes you draw!

This exercise can be structured. For example, if the children are looking at a variety of buildings, they could collect window shapes, followed by door and doorway shapes, followed by roof shapes and so on. It is important that they don't try to draw the whole building at this stage; they are still investigating and gaining experience of architectural shapes which will be invaluable as the project progresses. Ask children to look carefully for some of the smaller objects that are found on buildings. The shapes of alarms, grills, drainage pipes, aerials, satellite dishes, name plates, door furniture and much else can all be collected in their sketchbooks.

You will need: sketchbooks, or drawing boards and paper; drawing media.

Above: collecting shapes from outside the school building

Emphasising pattern, colour, texture, tone, lines and marks when looking at a building

As well as investigating different architectural shapes, children could also explore the other visual qualities they can see when looking at a building. For example, they could collect architectural patterns. Ask them to draw just enough of the pattern to be able to recognise it clearly as a pattern. There is no need to draw it all. Younger children might need to do some simple revision about repeating patterns. Look back at pages 22–25 in this book for more ideas about developing children's awareness of pattern.

Children could also try to mix some of the different colours they can see in the building or they could collect some of the textures by making rubbings or Plasticine prints. Ask them where they can see lines in the building. The children could practice drawing different

lines and then try out different marks to show textures. You might talk with children about the darkest parts of the building and then discuss the lightest parts they can see. Ask them where they can see shadows. Children could then make some quick tonal drawings of small sections of the building in their sketchbooks. There are examples on pages 43 and 55 of ways of helping children explore the concept of tone.

In all these examples of investigative work the emphasis is on exploring and experimenting, rather than making good-looking end products.

You will need: sketchbooks, or drawing boards and paper; drawing media appropriate to each investigation (use soft pastels to collect colours; use charcoal and chalk or soft drawing pencils to record tones; wax crayons may be needed to make rubbings of textures).

Top left: this child is making a sophisticated collection of shapes from the built environment. He has certainly taken on board the suggestion to draw shapes inside shapes

Top right: this collection of shapes is finished. Look at how this child started very simply with basic shapes and then became increasingly confident

Left: looking for shapes has helped this artist try to get to grips with the difficult task of drawing the gable end and roof lines of this domestic house in an estate that can be seen from the school playground

Session 3

Making an observational drawing of a building

You have decided which building or buildings the children are going to draw. It is important that they are comfortable when they are working outside, so they may need something to sit on. They will all need to be able to see the building clearly. If they want to make a larger drawing, you will need to use drawing boards. If there is any wind, use masking tape to hold the corners of the paper. Children can easily prepare their own boards in this way. Masking tape can be peeled off carefully at the end without tearing the drawing.

The children could use fibre-tipped pens (or hand-writing pens) because they will not be able to rub the ink out. Alternatives include black wax crayons, charcoal, even black biros. Drawing with materials like these is an effective strategy, if children are nervous about drawing and inclined to use rubbers a lot. Some children spend so much time rubbing out their mistakes that they hardly do any drawing at all! Here are some strategies to help children feel more confident about their drawing.

Talking about making mistakes

Who plays a musical instrument? What was it like when you first started learning? Did you make lots of mistakes? What did the tune you were playing sound like? Who has been playing a musical instrument for while? What is it like when you try to play a new piece for the first time? Do you still make mistakes? What do you need to do to get better? Practise?

Drawing is just the same. Even artists who have been drawing a long time make lots of mistakes, especially if it is a new way of drawing or if they are trying something they have not drawn before. Everybody makes mistakes. Don't worry about them too much.

If you think you have made a mistake at the start of your drawing, it can look dreadful and you will think, 'I have ruined my work already.' What you should do is forget about the mistake and keep going, because by the end of the drawing it will not look nearly as obvious.

There will always be parts of the drawing that you think look good and parts that you are not so pleased with. Your drawing will not be perfect. Although some people are better at drawing than others, everybody will improve if they practise. So, don't worry about your mistakes.

Such talk will not soothe the fear of drawing in every child straight away, but you will be promoting confidence and fluency. It is worth persevering with this approach and the fibre-tipped pens because, after a while, the children will become used to this way of working and quickly settle down to draw. When they have gained the confidence to draw fluently you could give them pencils to draw with again. The children will also enjoy your enthusiasm for their drawing even if it is not to your taste as an adult. A drawing might appear slap-dash at first glance but perhaps this child is drawing the building with great gusto. What seems slap-dash to one person could look like expressive energy to another. Consider how the child is approaching their drawing and what they say about it. Look out for your own aesthetic prejudices before judging work too harshly. There is also a discussion on page 62 about helping children feel confident about drawing.

Top: a finished drawing of buildings

Opposite left: this drawing was made with a soft drawing pencil. The artist was confident in his drawing and realised there was no need to rub out mistakes continually

Opposite right: this is a very different style of drawing. This child is as interested in the way her viewpoint is interrupted by shrubs and plants, as in the building itself. It was also a very windy morning

Starting the drawing

Find the middle of your paper. Look at the building. Find a shape near the middle of the building. Try starting the drawing by putting that first shape in the middle of the paper. Next, look for shapes that are near to the first one and add those to your drawing. Your drawing will grow bit by bit as you add in more of the shapes you can see. Don't forget that most of the shapes will have other shapes inside them. Think carefully about where each new shape should go. Only draw the outline shape of the whole building after you have drawn most of the important window and door shapes.

Another way to start the drawing

Use the pencil very lightly. Draw the shape of the whole building onto your paper. Think carefully about how big the building is going to look on the paper. Don't draw any detail with the pencil. The idea is that you are planning how the building is going to fit on the paper. You could add in one or two windows or a door. Think about how big the windows and doors should be and where they are going inside the main shape of the building. Remember, don't spend too long on the planning, there is no need to draw any detail with the pencil.

With this last strategy, children will need pencils and rubbers, but only to start with. If they are using large sheets of paper, you may need to ask them to think big. There may be more than one building or other things that they would like to include in the drawing and they could draw in the outline shapes of these, as well. When they are happy with how everything fits on the paper, collect up the pencils and rubbers and children can start to draw with fibre-tipped pens. Just as in the first example, encourage them to draw the smaller shapes, working in the middle of the drawing first. Tell them that

they will be able to rub out the pencil lines when they have finished. If you use this strategy it is important that the children do the minimum of pencil planning. It is simply to help them fit the drawing into the space of the paper.

Working on the drawing

Keep looking for all those shapes. Do you remember the patterns you found? You could add in some of the patterns, too.

Advanced children may well have done recent work with textures, tones and lines and marks. If you think it is appropriate, you could ask them to think about showing the dark parts of the building in their drawing, or they could add in any textures they can see, particularly the textures of the surface of the building itself. But for younger or less advanced children, it may be more than enough to concentrate on shape alone.

Finishing the drawing

Do children want to give their drawings a background? Have you talked with them about all that is in front of, above, behind or alongside the building? This involves talking about the space that surrounds the building, space being another of the basic visual concepts (see page 43 for ideas about drawing space in terms of foreground and background).

If you feel a child could work for longer on their drawing, ask them to look for extra shapes or patterns, particularly within the architectural details. Or encourage them to add more shapes and patterns from the area around the building.

You will need: sketchbooks, or drawing boards and paper; drawing media (see page 79).

Session 4

Drawing urban landscapes

The strategy outlined in the previous session can be used to help children draw an urban landscape full of different buildings. The emphasis in the discussion prior to drawing could be that there are many, many shapes within the view across town.

Children could begin by collecting the shapes of all the different buildings they can see (look at page 77). When they start to draw an urban environment, the most helpful method is to start in the middle of the paper with a shape and add others in turn to make a kind of patchwork of shapes as the drawing spreads across the paper.

Before drawing any landscape, experimental work on lines will also be useful (see page 15).

You will need: sketchbooks, or drawing boards and paper; drawing media.

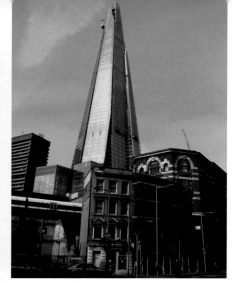

Session 5

Talking about buildings

Talking is a good starting point for the following chapter about architecture, as well as a progressive aspect of drawing buildings. You can talk about real buildings or buildings in reproduction (either as digital images or paper printouts and photographs). The best strategy is to have two or more buildings to compare. For example, a Victorian house compared with a modern home from an estate nearby; a Tudor fortified house compared with a Roman villa; a Jewish synagogue compared with a mosque and a church or chapel. You could look at public and private buildings, industrial buildings compared with shops, or you could talk about two or more well known buildings from the locality. The children could also compare the buildings that they use and live in with buildings from different countries and cultures.

The following sequence of questions falls into roughly four groups. Although this is described in a way that is suitable for whole class discussion, why not ask groups of children to talk about similar questions written down for them in advance? They could go on to compose a more formal piece of writing about buildings.

• *Tell me, what can you see when you look at the front of this building?*

In each case, ask the children this very simple question. Encourage them to mention all the obvious things as well as the more subtle points. A group of children will always find far more to talk about than one person will ever think of on their own. A good strategy is to keep a list of what the children say. It can provide a very useful prompt for describing the building in more detail later.

• *Talk about the shapes, patterns, colours or textures you can you see.*

You could work through shape, pattern, colour and texture in turn. The children could simply talk about what they can see or they could link the discussion with a practical activity. They could collect shapes or patterns as on page 22. They could mix the colours they can see in different buildings. They could collect some of the surface textures of different building materials by taking rubbings or Plasticine prints, they could experiment with different drawing media to try and find marks that show the different textures.

• *How does this building make you feel? What happens in this building? Who uses this building? How is the building used?*

These questions are about establishing the character of each building. It is a way of discussing what values the architecture might communicate. Here are some more suggestions along the same lines:

• *As you stand in front of this building, what impression do you get? How does the building make you feel? Is this feeling different from the other building we looked at? How? What would you think if you used this building every day? What would it be like to live in this building? What about windows and doorways, are they different from the ones you have at home? How are they different? Does the building remind you of anything else? Talk about the different characters of the buildings we have looked at together.*

Next ask the children for their opinions about the building.

• *What do you like and dislike about it? Which of the buildings we have been discussing do you prefer? Can you say why?*

This will prompt the children to make value judgments about the buildings under discussion. It is interesting to begin talking about buildings with questions like this and then to repeat them at the end of the discussion. Have any of the children changed their minds? Some of the most exciting discussions are with children who hold opposite points of view and are prepared to argue for them.

All the work on drawing buildings could be adapted as an introduction to the architecture project described in the next chapter.

You will need: The actual buildings themselves; digital images to project or paper-based images.

Below: a collage made by children at Peteson Super Ely Church in Wales Primary School *working with Julie Ashfield*

9

Architecture

Session 1

Designing a building in elevation

Children should have experienced or revised some of the foundation exercises on pages 66 and 67. They may have made an observational drawing of a building or urban landscape (see pages 78–81). The following sequence of activities should help them design an elevation for an imaginative building of their own.

An internet or library search

The library will contain many books that have images of buildings. Ask the children to search for the best examples. General reference books, history and geography books are obvious places to start looking. Story books, graphic novels and books for younger children can also have excellent illustrations of imaginary buildings. You may want the children to focus on a particular period in history, or perhaps a particular part of the world. Other possibilities include focusing on places of worship, domestic houses and homes, or imaginary buildings. Children might categorise some examples they find under headings that emerge from the discussion about the various purposes or functions of buildings.

Searching via the internet will also yield a wealth of images. How can children define their search terms to get worthwhile results? Searching for 'temples' will produce a rich variety of images of temples from all around the world and historical eras. By searching for the term 'Buddhist temples', children will refine their results. 'Buddhist temples in India' will yield even more specific images. The next section is about collecting examples of window, door and roof shapes. So, children might try 'windows in Buddhist temples'. With a potentially limitless access to source material, learning to research and collect ideas for use in an art and design project is an important skill to develop. Of course, your school, local authority or school board will have policies in place about the safe and appropriate use of the internet.

You will need: the school library (supplement this project with books from the local library or from home); internet access and laptop computers.

Collecting examples of window, door and roof shapes

First of all, collect lots of examples of the different window shapes you have found. You may need to draw in some of the smaller shapes that make the inside shapes of the window. Then collect some door and doorway shapes and then some roof shapes. Remember that the idea is to collect lots of different kinds of windows, doors and roofs so don't spend too long on any one drawing.

This exercise could be structured so that different groups research a different aspect; one group collects window shapes, another collects door and doorway shapes and so on. Or perhaps different children within each group could have the responsibility for collecting examples from one or other of the categories. These categories could be extended or reorganised to take into account buildings from different continents or different periods in history.

You will need: books with photographs and illustrations of buildings (from the school library, the local library or from home); internet access and laptop computers; a printer to make paper copies of images.

Top left: these children warmed up by inventing their own shapes

Top right: collecting architectural shapes by researching books in the library. Imaginative buildings from illustrated stories can also be a very valid starting point

Below: using printouts of some of the images the children found on the internet. These were stored in plastic wallets with their shape ideas and first architectural experiments. All this material is a valuable resource as the design process continues

Right: talking about buildings and their uses can be a helpful link to other areas of the curriculum, such as R.E. This is a detail of Gaudi's Sagrada Familia in Barcelona

Below: using a digital camera as a tool to help collect ideas and record information is an important skill for any design project. Is it possible to organise a walk or a trip out of school to look at examples of architecture?

Session 2

Using a camera to record architectural details from local buildings

The previous exercise could be repeated or extended to include examples collected from photographs of windows, doors and roofs taken from buildings local to the school, or perhaps from interesting and varied architecture in a local town or city. Children enjoy taking their own photographs and this is an opportunity to give basic instruction in using a digital camera. Further research using photographs could involve collecting examples of patterns, textures and other details or features in architecture. The children could draw examples or even use the photocopier to make individual collections of visual information about buildings from the wide range of images taken by the whole group or class. Printouts and photocopies can be cut up and collaged and then enhanced further with drawing and written notes.

You will need: camera; local examples of different buildings and architectural styles; sketchbooks, or drawing boards and paper; drawing media; photocopier; computers and a printer.

Session 3

Talking about different kinds of buildings and their uses

Why do we need buildings? What are buildings for? What different kinds of buildings are there? What happens inside different buildings? Why are buildings so different one from another? What kinds of buildings are there near the school or near where you live? How could you tell just by looking at a building what it is used for? What kinds of buildings do we live in? What are some of the features that make the school building different from the building you live in? What are some of the differences between a factory and a church? Have you ever been inside any unusual or particularly interesting kinds of buildings?

It may be useful to make a record of some of the important points that come out of this discussion. A list of all the different categories of buildings will help children make decisions about the type of building they would like to design.

What you will need: images of different buildings and architectural styles

Deciding what kind of building to design

There are some choices to be made. Are the children going to be free to design any kind of building they choose? If the project is closely connected to a particular theme, you may decide that the designs should be for hospitals, factories, castles, Roman temples, places of worship, domestic houses, or maybe for imaginary buildings for characters in a story or novel. The buildings might be designed as part of a story children have written themselves. Whatever the choice, this is a rich opportunity for further discussion and sharing ideas. The idea of a building could be extended to include special places. For example, perhaps the place children design is a series of subterranean tunnels and caves for people who live underground.

Top left and right: collaboration can be a feature of this project. Children begin to discuss ideas about their own building. These children are making both written and visual notes

Looking at an architect's drawing

Looking at an architect's drawing might prompt a discussion about different types of drawings and what they are used for. An architect produces drawings for other contractors to use. Architects also produce drawings to give a client an idea about what the finished building will look like in the context of its site. Artists, on the other hand, produce very different kinds of drawings of buildings, either real or imaginary.

What kind of people need to look at an architect's drawing? Let's make a list of the different people who will be involved in building a house to an architect's designs.

Most local architects will be only too pleased to lend or give you copies of their old drawings and plans. Ask for an example of an elevation. You may want to discuss with children the site plans and maps which show the blueprint of a building and its location in relation to surrounding buildings and natural features. There are good links to be made here with map-making and scale drawing. If you have more than one elevation to look at, you can make comparisons. There might also be an opportunity to invite an architect into the classroom to meet the children or even for a visit to an architect's office. Architects' models can provide the stimulus for work in three dimensions following this design project.

Talking about an elevation for a building drawn by a real architect will help the children understand how to work on their own drawing. But it is important that the children have their own ideas and do not simply copy an adult approach.

You will need: architects' drawings and plans; a visit to an architect's office or perhaps an invitation to an architect to visit the school.

Top: are you able to borrow an architect's drawing to show the children? This drawing shows the blueprint of a contemporary home

Above: these boys are starting their design with pencils. Notice that much of the resource material is still available for ideas

Opposite: these ten year olds readily accepted the challenge of working on a large scale as they set about designing a building

Sessions 4 and 5

Talking about how to get started on a design

You have gathered lots of information and ideas. You have books from the library and photographs. We have talked a lot about different kinds of buildings. You should have decided what kind of building you are going to design. You only need to think about the front of the building, the elevation, just like the elevations in the architects' drawings we looked at together. Choose what shapes of windows and what shapes of doors or entrances look right for your building. What is the roof going to be like? How many windows will there be? How many doors are needed? How big is your building? How big are the windows and doors? What other things will you need to include? Think about what the building is used for. How would people who use the building like it to look?

You may wish to focus children on an entirely imaginative idea. For example, after looking at Italian villas, you could encourage them in this way:

Remember what you said about these buildings. They were magnificent, splendid, huge, amazing, stylish, rich, wonderful, awe-inspiring. Now, when you are thinking about the design of your own building, try to make sure that it looks magnificent, grand, splendid, huge, amazing, palatial, stylish, rich, wonderful, awe-inspiring...

Ask the children to think about ornamentation to enhance their building.

You will need: the collections of drawings, images and ideas children have made; books, printouts, or digital images saved in accessible files.

Drawing the design in pencil first

At this stage, one approach would be to ask children to work in rough to try out a number of ideas before committing themselves. However, the class may be so full of ideas that they want to get on with their designs right away. Planning in advance is good design practice, but it can inhibit children's natural and spontaneous creativity. Are they bursting to get on with their designs? Is it possible to offer some children the chance to work more slowly and carefully making rough plans, if they so choose?

Children will be working on large sheets of paper: A2 is ideal. It will be much easier for them if they have drawing boards. Give them HB pencils and tell them they can use any equipment that will help, including rulers, set squares, compasses and even rubbers! Ask them to work lightly in pencil first because they may need to rub out quite a lot of their drawing before they have a design that they are pleased with.

They should be encouraged to stop from time to time to look calmly at their work and discuss it with their colleagues around the table. You may feel it is appropriate to have small teams of children – say three or four per group – who are working together on a larger design. It is very important that children can refer easily to their ideas, images, photographs and any other relevant visual information. Remind them about all the possibilities for windows, doors, roofs, patterns and details.

Children may find it difficult if they draw a large outline of their building first. Sometimes they have difficulty filling this large shape with coherent architectural features. A good approach to help with this compositional problem is to mirror the advice on drawing portraits and landscapes: start from the centre and work towards the outside of the building.

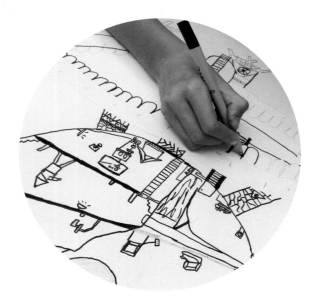

Left and opposite: a design process such as this architecture project is valuable on many levels. Children who work in this way are learning to be creative, collaborative problem-solvers, open-minded enquirers and critical thinkers

Children only need think about the outline after the majority of the main architectural ideas are in place.

You will need: sketchbooks, or drawing boards and paper; drawing media including HB pencils; rulers; compasses; set squares; rubbers; in these photographs, some children worked on large rolls of paper 1.2 m wide.

Finishing the design in ink and adding details

Are you happy with your designs? Have one last look. Is there anything you would like to change? If you have finished, you should now draw over your pencil lines in ink. You can use the thin fibre-tipped pens. When you have inked up your drawing you can rub out all the pencil marks.

The architects' drawings that the children looked at may have included other details such as trees or drawings of people to give a sense of scale. The children could add these details to their designs. Ask them to look carefully at the way the architects drew the extra details and to try to add them into their drawings in the same way. If the building is for an imaginary character from a story or novel, then the extra details could be imaginatively derived from the story.

This design project does not include work on colour or texture. However, children could go on to consider appropriate colours and textures for their design, and link these to the materials from which the building could be made. There is a lot of potential work here on building materials and building techniques and a technological focus could become a powerful part of the design project.

You could extend the project even further by constructing the elevation in card. Perhaps a whole set of elevations could make a table-top town or street.

This extension to the project can also be linked to making stage and film sets.

Why not consider a room or rooms in the building? What kind of fabrics could be used for carpets, curtains and furniture? What would the furniture be like and how would it be arranged? What would the colour scheme be like?

This work on interiors links well to the pattern design project on pages 22–29.

You will need: thin card or large sheets of paper; rubbers; thin felt or fibre-tipped pens (handwriting pens); drawing and colouring materials.

Talking about the architecture project and display

Leave the architectural drawings on the tabletops or drawing boards. Prop the boards along a corridor or around the walls of the classroom or hall.

Look carefully at all the designs. Choose a design that you think works well, that looks good. Try to think of a reason for your decision. You might find it difficult to say why you liked the drawing you chose. A good way of finding out more about a design is to interview the architect. What questions could you ask?

Display examples of all the work alongside the finished architectural drawings. The photographs, printouts, books, photocopied pages from sketchbooks and observational drawings from the previous project on drawing buildings will support the child's growing understanding of the design process.

You will need: all the children's work from this and other projects related to buildings.

10

Clay tiles and sculptural relief

Session 1

Introducing children to ceramic tiles and sculptural relief

This is an art and design project where there are specific skills and techniques to learn. It is a good idea to begin by demonstrating how the finished tiles or plaques will be made. This will help children understand how the various parts of the project link together and how the chosen technique will necessarily influence the way they work right from the start. If you have never taught this type of project before, then the very best approach is to set aside some time to try out the procedures yourself. Read through this chapter for guidance. Children will need to be shown the clay and the tools and equipment. It is worth demonstrating how to roll a slab of clay, how to cut and trim these slabs, how to use slip, how to make the lines and shapes they will use to build up a relief and how to take care of the clay and the finished tiles.

The term 'relief' is used in sculpture to describe how sculpted material is raised above a flat base or background. There are examples of sculptural relief from all historical epochs. Try an internet search using the term 'relief', together: with 'sculpture', 'sculptural', 'ceramic' or 'clay'. This is an opportunity to explain the difference between removing material to create an image (carving) and building up an image from a base or ground by adding material. It is this latter process which children will use to make their clay tiles or plaques.

Top right: using different drawing media to explore line

Bottom right: an informal exhibition of work offers a chance to talk and share ideas

Warming up by drawing lines

The following sequence of activities will help children to learn the technique of making a ceramic relief plaque or tile. Most importantly it will also illustrate how artists and designers often look to their immediate environment for ideas. The visual world around us is a rich and exciting treasure trove of stimuli and you can help children understand that it is always available as a catalyst for art and design. For this project, children were asked to use the myriad of lines that can be seen in the winter trees which back onto the school playground. Before going outside, warm up with activities to open up their sensibility to line.

First of all, we are going to experiment making a range of different lines. You have a number of different drawing media to use. But before you start, let's think about how lines can look. Help me make a list of words that we could use to describe a line.

Children will soon get the idea and suggest simple words such as zigzag, bent, curved, straight, long, and short. This is an opportunity to extend vocabulary. How about words such as, delicate, shaky, agitated, calm, wandering? Lines can also be fast, timid or extravagant! Children could make movements or sounds to help illustrate these sensations, feelings and qualities. Invite children to experiment making a range of lines with different media. Ask them not only to think in a literal way (that is, thinking of a word and inventing a line to go with it), but also invite them to see what happens when they create new lines simply by exploring (by not knowing what the line will look like in advance).

Investigating the environment around the school

Now you have created a huge number of different kinds of lines, let's go outside. Remember, our theme is 'trees in winter'. If you look at the trees and bushes at the back of the playground, you will discover that they are made up of countless different kinds of lines. I would like you to divide your sheet of paper in half. On one half, divide the paper again into four sections. Leave the other half empty. First of all, in the four small sections, make four different drawings looking at the trees and bushes from different places. We call this 'drawing from different viewpoints'. Afterwards, choose one spot and make a larger drawing. Remember, we are only really interested in the lines. You do not have to draw a whole tree and your tree does not have to look realistic.

We are also going to collect some of the details of the trees and bushes from different viewpoints using a camera. Everyone will have a chance to take two or three photographs. You will be using the photographs and the drawings to help you design a motif for a clay plaque.

Top left: working in sketchbooks outside and collecting ideas from various viewpoints. It is important that the children have the opportunity to move around

Top right: using cameras to record the lines in the trees

Right: a selection of finished drawings and designs

Session 2

Making clay tiles and practising making a motif on a single tile

Remind children both about clay and the equipment they will be using. Lay two wooden slats of even thickness parallel to each other on a wooden board. The distance between the slats will be the width of the tile. You may wish to glue or screw the slats in position. The length of the slats should be the same. This helped the children trim the clay so that each tile was a rectangle of similar size. Use a rolling pin to roll out a lump of clay. The rolling pin should be wider than the distance between the slats. Children may need to press more clay into any gaps that appear and re-roll their slab. The smooth, flat slab can now be trimmed.

Now you can practise making a clay tile of your own. As this is a practice we will cut the rectangle in half. The first half is the practice plaque itself, the base. You will cut lines and shapes out of the second half so as to make the relief. Look at the photos and your drawings. Use the lines to help you make a motif on your tile. Don't forget you will need to use the slip to fix each clay line on your tile. Remember this is a practice tile.

The children will learn a lot about the problems during this exercise. The emphasis is on practising making the slabs, rather than on the quality of the designs. Save some time to talk about the problems the children encountered.

You will need: all the equipment needed for using clay (clay, either buff-colured or red earthenware; plastic food bags to keep the clay moist; wooden boards for children to work on; clay tools; damp sponges and an old towel); wood for boards to help make tiles; photographs and photocopies of preparatory drawings

Above: rolling out a slab of clay

Left: designing plaques by laying out lines and shapes. Children are exploring various alternatives and using slip to fix each line or shape firmly onto the base. It is best to score the back of the line so that the slip grips really well. Slip is a mixture of clay and water. A good consistency is like double cream

Below: applying a light, even pressure with the rolling pin will help the shapes adhere to the base and smooth the surface

Designing and making the plaque

Now that children understand some of the problems involved in making relief images on clay tiles, they will be better able to think about designs. Invite them to work on paper to draw out possible ideas into rectangles that have the same proportion as the finished plaques. As an alternative, pupils can design by cutting out a variety of different lines and shapes from the spare clay slab and arranging them in various configurations on the plaque. If they are working in this way, ask them not to use any slip until they are completely happy with the finished arrangement. They can then work patiently to fix each line firmly onto the base with slip.

The children in these photographs worked in twos and threes on the plaques. Most decided to design the reliefs using the second alternative above. There is always a judgment to be made about whether to let children start making or whether to insist on a design process. For some children, designing on paper can inhibit their natural and spontaneous creativity, for others, designing on paper will help them slow down and consider their ideas more carefully. However, many children learn best working with the material. A camera is a useful tool. If children are exploring different arrangements with the clay, ask them to take a photograph of at least two different ideas. These can be talked about when reviewing the final work. In this way, they will begin to see how designing helps to form ideas in a useful way.

You will need: all the equipment needed for using clay (see page 97); wood for boards to help make tiles; photographs and photocopies of preparatory drawings.

Right: about half way through the activity it is helpful to stop and talk about problems and possibilities. The clay tools are on the table because Mrs Ashfield is going to suggest how lines and patterns could be incised onto the relief

Below: learning about different clay tools and how they can help the work

Right and opposite: plaques are left to dry. These abstract motifs would combine well to make a larger ceramic relief

Session 3

Making a larger ceramic relief with the tiles

Here is a brief guide to how to make a larger ceramic relief sculpture or mural. First of all, ask children to think about the size and shape of the mural. You may want them to make a scale drawing. Ask them to draw a rectangle that represents the shape of the whole relief to scale. Take the class back to their investigations and ask them to include in their design, drawings of everything that might be important features. The project illustrated here has lines inspired by trees in winter as its theme, but this technique is appropriate for any subject matter.

You may wish to ask other people to help give the children a design brief. Perhaps the parents or governors should have a say about the designs. The head teacher may point out that the money for all the materials is being paid for by the school, so he or she should give the children the brief. Why not invite one group to write a design brief for another? They will be in a client/contractor relationship. What does the artist who will design and make the relief need to know? What are the constraints? What is the theme or subject of the work? Why has this theme been chosen by the client?

Groups of children can discuss their ideas before designing. If there is time after they have finished their first design, ask them to have another go, making any changes or improvements, or perhaps starting on a completely new idea.

Decide together on the points you might look for when considering whether a design is good or not. Lay out the possibilities on the tables and put a letter or number by each. Ask children to choose their three favourite designs. They could write the letter of their chosen design on a slip of paper, fold the paper and post it into a ballot box. Count up which three designs have the most votes. Now repeat the process with the three favourites to choose the winning design.

The design could be drawn to scale on a large sheet of paper (A1). Divide up the small design into squares or rectangles. If it is too small, enlarge it on the photocopier. Each square or rectangle should represent the scale size of one of the clay tiles that will make up the relief. A small group of able children can tackle this, although they may need some help. It is also possible to add to or change the winning design at this stage.

Children can work in small groups to make one of the squares or rectangles for the relief using the process outlined in this chapter. When all the individual relief slabs have been made, they can be assembled into the final sculpture.

If you are going to keep this work permanently the slabs will need firing. Most schools will not have a kiln. Why not contact your local secondary or high school? Or perhaps a college with an art department can help? You will need advice about glazing and mounting the finished tiles onto a wall or board.

A small-scale ceramic tiled mural could be made for the classroom using the same process outlined above, but with fewer tiles. It is possible to leave the tiles unfired, but remind children that the clay will be very fragile when dry and seal each tile with PVA glue (mixed half and half with water) before painting, rather than glazing. You can use a strong glue to fix the tiles to a wooden board for display.

You will need: all the equipment for using clay (see page 97); wood for boards to help make tiles; rolling pins; photographs and photocopies of preparatory drawings; paper and drawing media to make the finished design to scale.

11

Visiting art

Session 1

Preparing for a visit to a gallery

Contact the gallery you wish to visit. Do you need to book your visit? Is there an education officer? Are there any organised projects or activities that you could link with? Are there any special restrictions about the number of children you can take or what activities are allowed when you are there? For example, some galleries will only allow children to work with clipboards or sketchbooks and pencils. Others may have a full programme of workshops and a studio space.

If you are taking the children yourself, it is helpful to visit the gallery first to find out about the facilities and what is on show. The gallery visit should be part of a wider project that includes work in the classroom.

Left and right: visiting art might mean going to a local art gallery or museum. Here children are at the Sainsbury Centre at the University of East Anglia in Norwich. Many galleries, including this one, offer extensive education programmes and will often work closely with you to plan the content of a visit

Starting with a look around the exhibition

When the children first see the exhibition, they are naturally curious and want to look around. Is it possible to give them a few minutes to explore the exhibition space? Ask them to look out for something particular. For example, ask the children to think about the different people they can see in the paintings. You will need to have an appropriate number of adults to accompany a class. Although supervision in a public space is an issue, try to give the children a chance to orientate themselves and investigate the room they are in before they settle down to more focused work.

Talking about the gallery

Bring the children together to talk. Sit the children on the floor. Ask them to comment on general things first.

What are your first impressions of the gallery? What do you think of this exhibition? What have you noticed so far? You were looking out for different people in the portraits. What have you seen?

Talking about a specific art object

Discuss with children the possibilities for more focused work. Can the groups agree which art object they are going to look at more carefully? Each group could talk about one work of art in the gallery in detail. Children could use ideas from the discussion and any drawing and note-taking they may do to help develop artwork back at school.

Children will find it helpful if there is a structure to support these conversations. Four broad areas may help them to enhance the quality of their talk: what there is to see, visual qualities and materials, meaning, and opinion.

Talk about what you can see when you look at the artwork. Sometimes it is helpful to make a list. Mention all the obvious things as well as those intriguing details. For example, the sculpture may be made of wood. That might seem obvious but it is still important to mention it. Mention everything you can see, even if you don't know what it is or don't know what it means.

Now think about the visual qualities you can see. For example, can you talk about all the colours or the textures? Are there patterns? What about the size of the object? Is there sense of space (what is furthest away from you or closest to you)?

The following are questions which will help children develop a more sophisticated critical language to talk about art objects. This kind of talk will benefit from adult mediation.

You can now think about what the artwork might mean – what it might be saying. For example, you could ask: what is happening? Imagine what might happen next. If there is a person depicted, what do you imagine are they thinking about or feeling? Why do you think the artwork looks the way it does? If you could meet the artist what do you think they would say? Do you think this work of art tells us anything about the kind of person who made it?

Lastly, talk about your opinions. For example, do you like the art? What do you like about it? What do you dislike? Remember, it's fine both to like and dislike different aspects of the same work of art. If you could, would you like to take this work of art home and have it in your bedroom? What are your reasons? How does it compare with others you have seen? Regardless of your own opinion, what do you think other people will think of this art?

Session 2

Drawing, photographing and making notes about works of art in public places

These records and investigations will be useful for work back at school. Can you support children with advice about using a camera? For example, can photographs be taken close to a work of art to show detail? From above? From a more distant viewpoint so that more of the surroundings are shown? Are children able to review their photographs on the camera and decide if they need alternative shots? Similar criteria might be applied to drawings. Notes might be linked to the kinds of questions suggested in the previous section.

Above and opposite: researching the Merchant Seafarer's Memorial outside the Welsh Assembly building in Cardiff. The children were asked to take into account the site and setting for this sculpture. Why was it made? Why is it sited here?

Bottom left: this is another view of the same sculpture. It is really important that children have time to look at three-dimensional work from a number of different angles and viewpoints

Bottom right: this part of Cardiff Bay is a great place to visit because there are so many site-specific sculptures within a small area. Art is often a feature of public buildings and public places. You might not need to go very far to find good examples for this kind of project. Cameras are a vital tool for recording information and ideas

Session 3

Developing ideas about making art inspired by visiting artwork

Children will return to the classroom with a wealth of experiences, ideas, drawings, notes and photographs. Here you can see how all these can be combined to create ideas sheets which are environments for forming ideas about creating artwork of their own.

Top left: using collage techniques to cut out and glue ideas onto the sheets. It is always useful if children have access to a photocopier and/or a computer and printer as they can crop, re-size and digitally alter some of the raw material

Top right: working together in pairs or threes to create ideas sheets. Pupils used all the material gathered on the visit. These included notes, photographs, drawings, printed information plus their memories and recollections of the art and the immediate vicinity

Below: working in this way, children can create a wealth of visual ideas. Which of these concepts could be developed into sculptural maquettes (models for sculptures)?

Opposite: as they worked, children were invited to create ideas for a site-specific sculpture of their own. What would you make if you were an artist who was invited to make a sculpture for this area? Where would you site it? What would it be made of? What would be your chosen theme?

12

Relief printing and constructing with cardboard

Session 1

Starting points for relief printing

This block or relief printing project is another example where a particular process and technique is important. Just as in making a ceramic sculptural relief, it is advisable to take time to become familiar with the process before showing children. A good way to start this work is to demonstrate how children will be making the print before starting the project. This will give purpose and direction to the preparatory work. Children will also understand why some approaches will produce better results than others, and will adapt their designs accordingly.

Children could begin work by developing ideas for pattern (see page 22), or by researching the natural environment in the same way as for the sculptural reliefs on page 96. Alternatively, motifs and images for the prints could come from visual ideas sheets on any number of themes (see page 106). Ideas for prints can be stimulated by experiments with visual qualities such as shape, line and pattern (see pages 40–45). Examples of adult abstract art could also provide an inspiration. For example, twentieth century artists such as Kandinsky, Klee, Albers, Riley, Rothko, Dubuffet, Pasmore, and Nicholson use shape in abstract two-dimensional work. This is just a representative list; there may well be a local artist whose abstract painting and drawing could become a focus for the children's print-making. Non-representational art from different cultures could also be used as a stimulus for this work.

This print-making process contrasts with the sculptural techniques used in the second part of this chapter. Teachers may want to use such juxtaposition to draw attention to differences between working in two and three dimensions. Planning two related projects in this way (say within the same half-term) will make it apparent to children just how different the processes used are, even though the basic material is the same (in this case, it is scrap corrugated card). Each process has its own characteristics, problems, positive and negative points.

The children in the photographs kept their work in large wallets made from strong, clear plastic, stapled onto stiff cardboard. They were able to look back on previous work for ideas.

Your pattern and shape collections stored in your wallets include many different kinds of shape. Divide a sheet of paper into four separate areas. I have put a selection of bases (blocks) on each table. First of all, use these bases as templates to draw around so that you have the correct shape of the base on your paper. Now you can draw ideas for a motif which you will be able to repeat again and again to make a printed pattern on a large sheet of paper. This is preparatory work for your print. Try several different ideas. Remember the demonstration of the block printing process? Who could talk about some of the problems you might find?

Right: this block is ready to be sealed with PVA glue before printing

Bottom left: children have cut shapes from the thin corrugated card and are using PVA to glue the shapes onto the blocks

Bottom right: the blocks don't have to be rectangular

Session 2

Making the relief blocks

You are going to make a relief print using a piece of medium-density fibreboard for the base. You can cut more shapes to make the motif in relief out of the corrugated cardboard. These will be glued onto the block.

You must now decide on your final design. You will need to cut out the shapes you are going to glue onto your block out of the corrugated cardboard. Arrange the shapes you cut out on the block. Until you have made your first print you will not know quite how it will turn out, so feel free to experiment with different arrangements based on your design.

When you are happy with the composition, you can glue the shapes and lines down with PVA glue. Use the PVA to coat the relief block, with the shapes glued on. This seals the block you are going to use to make the print. Leave the printing block to dry.

Children can use one cut-out shape as a template, if they want to repeat the same shape a number of times. You may need to explain what a template is. It is important that the workspace is well organised.

Look at pages 37–38, where a technique for using glue is described. This is similar. Here is a reminder.

You must think carefully about how you are going to organise your work space. Printing can be messy. If you are disorganised you are more likely to make mistakes. Decide on a dirty area and a clean area. You can use masking tape to tape a dividing line across the table to remind you. On the dirty side of the line will be the printing ink, trays to roll out the ink, rollers, sheets of newsprint or an old magazine, a damp sponge and a rag. On the clean side is the paper for your print.

Every time you roll out ink onto your block, you should do this on a clean sheet of newspaper. It is inevitable that ink will get onto the newspaper, so before you make the next print, put down a clean sheet. In this way you will be able to keep the dirty side of your work area as clean as possible.

Make the print on the paper, which should always stay on the clean side of the line. You can use a damp sponge and rag to keep your fingers clean. The inky roller must always stay in the tray.

Making the prints

First of all, you will need to choose a colour and roll out some ink onto this plastic tray. You can only roll out one colour on the block. We can talk about how to make multi-coloured prints later. Roll out the ink onto the block. Cover all one side of the block: the side with the raised shapes. Press the block onto your paper to make a print. Use the palm of your hand to press down firmly. Peel the block off the paper and look at your print. You are bound to need some help, so team up with a partner so you can help each other with the prints. Try different-coloured papers and make a series of prints from the same block.

The children will find it easier to print in pairs so that they can help each other. There are many variations to this basic activity. For example, a brush could be used to apply different-coloured inks to different raised shapes. Or, when the prints and the blocks are dry, the children could try a new colour ink on their block and overprint the colour onto the paper. They could apply the second colour to selected parts of the block only, or remove shapes from the block before they print the second colour. This will create a contrast between the two colours in the final outcome.

You can make larger class or group prints using this technique. Children can contribute different shapes and ideas to a much larger picture or design. Shapes can be used to create many different designs and pictures. Why not try prints that link to other areas of the curriculum? Once the children have learnt this technique and discovered some of the possibilities, they will be able to make relief prints with varied subject matter. For example, the prints might have an Aztec theme. Or, how about prints on the theme of fire, air and water? Children will cut out shapes and lines for flames, planes, clouds, waves, boats and much else besides. The arrangement of shapes on the block is one way to introduce ideas about composition.

Talking about and reviewing the finished work

Is there time to talk about the children's finished work? Storage of finished work is always a problem, especially as work needs time to dry. The easiest solution is to clear a display board in the classroom. Use drawing pins to pin up each print the children finish. This kind of display is very exciting. Call the board 'work in progress'. The children can see the prints clearly and can review what they have done and talk about the problems. Drawing boards may also be useful here. Clip prints to the boards as children finish, and prop the work up around the walls or along a corridor. This makes an informal exhibition. Again, children can see and discuss their own work and that of other children in the class. Talk about the problems they encountered, ways to improve the processes they used and how the final prints look. Artists often use a line strung up across the studio or workshop. Prints can be pegged to the line to dry.

You will need: paper and drawing media; fibre board blocks of different sizes (you can also use thick strong card such as strawboard); corrugated card; scissors; PVA; glue spreaders; brushes; water-based printing inks; flat trays for rolling out the ink; a cover for the tables (in the photographs we used sheets of hardboard cut to the size of the classroom tables); damp rags or sponges; old newspaper or magazines; rollers; paper to print on.

Top left: printing the final motif: these girls succeeded in making a regular pattern by being particularly careful where to make each successive print. They developed a technique of making tiny marks on the paper with a pencil – register marks – to help them place the block accurately

Top right: using a brush rather than a roller to apply paint to the relief

Overleaf: the relief printing process from start to finish

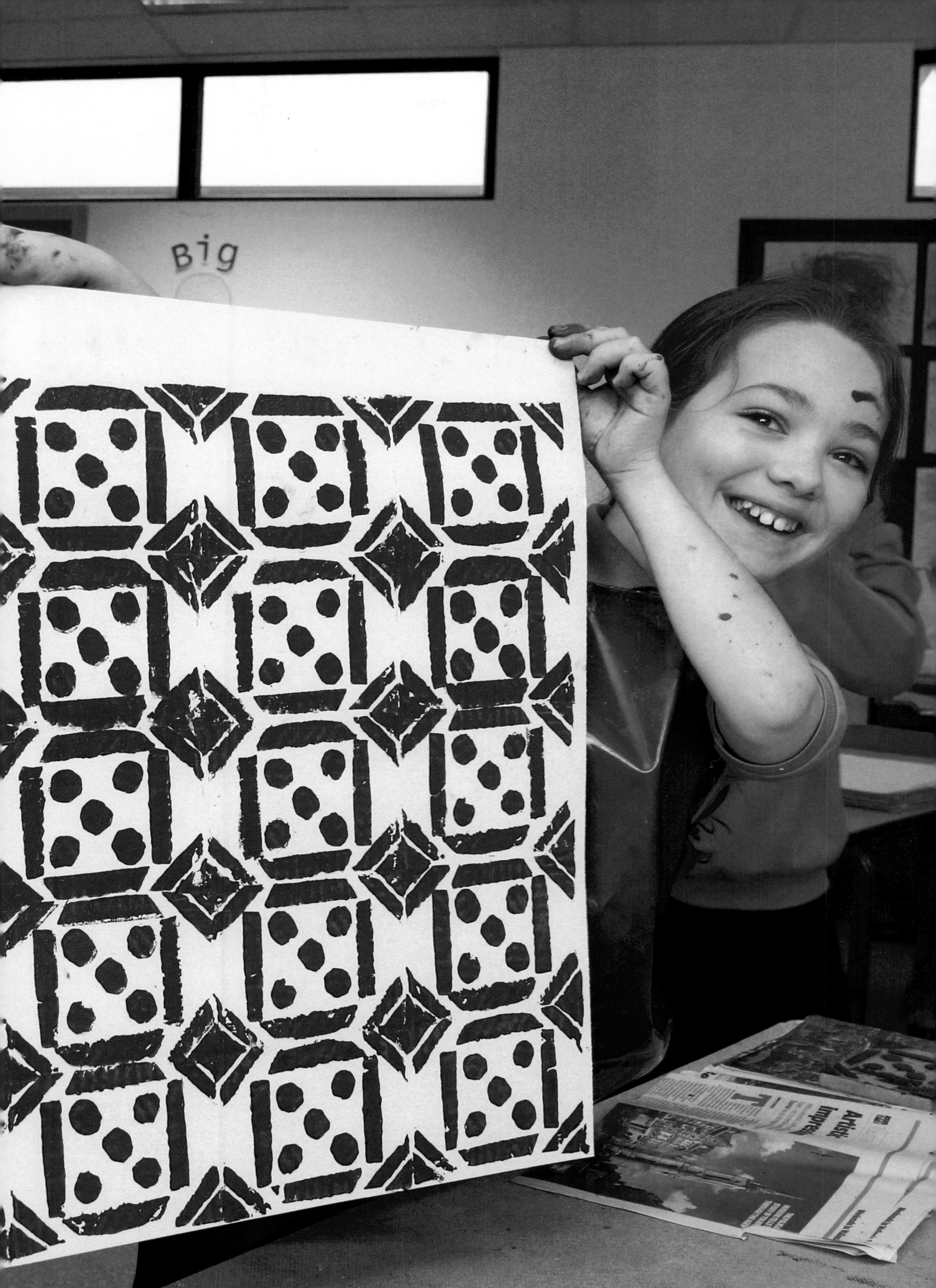
Big

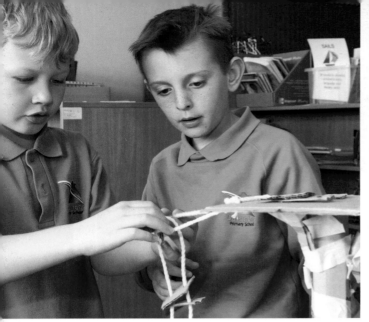

Session 3

Starting points for making cardboard constructions

Before children make a sculpture (or a construction) from cardboard, let them explore various basic techniques without any pressure to make anything. Here are some ideas:

You have some cardboard, some scissors, a hole punch, paper fasteners, masking tape, string and glue. I want you to experiment to find out as many different ways as you can, using these tools and materials, to join two or more pieces of cardboard together. At the end we will share all your ideas. Remember, we are working in three dimensions!

Children will discover a great deal by exploring in this way. In the review, try to make sure that everyone sees these basic techniques: making slits so that two pieces slot together; making tabs; plaiting and weaving one piece into another; punching holes and joining with string or paper fasteners (paper fasteners can be used rather like rivets); binding with string or tape; rolling into tubes (if the cardboard is thin enough), securing the tubes with masking tape and joining tubes together in different ways. Tubes make very strong struts.

To augment this starter activity, see if children can turn flat (two-dimensional) pieces of cardboard into self-supporting, three-dimensional forms. Here, look out for and encourage children who are folding, pleating, scoring, bending, tucking, etc.

You will need: cardboard; scissors; a hole punch; paper fasteners; masking tape; string; cloth; glue.

Making constructions

These photographs show children following a project from *Creativity and Culture – Art Projects for Primary Schools*. They have been creating imaginary communities. Part of the project led children to discussing the kinds of structures these imaginary people might live in. Following the introductory activity outlined in this section, children worked in pairs.

Top left, right, above and opposite: dwellings created after exploring a number of construction techniques

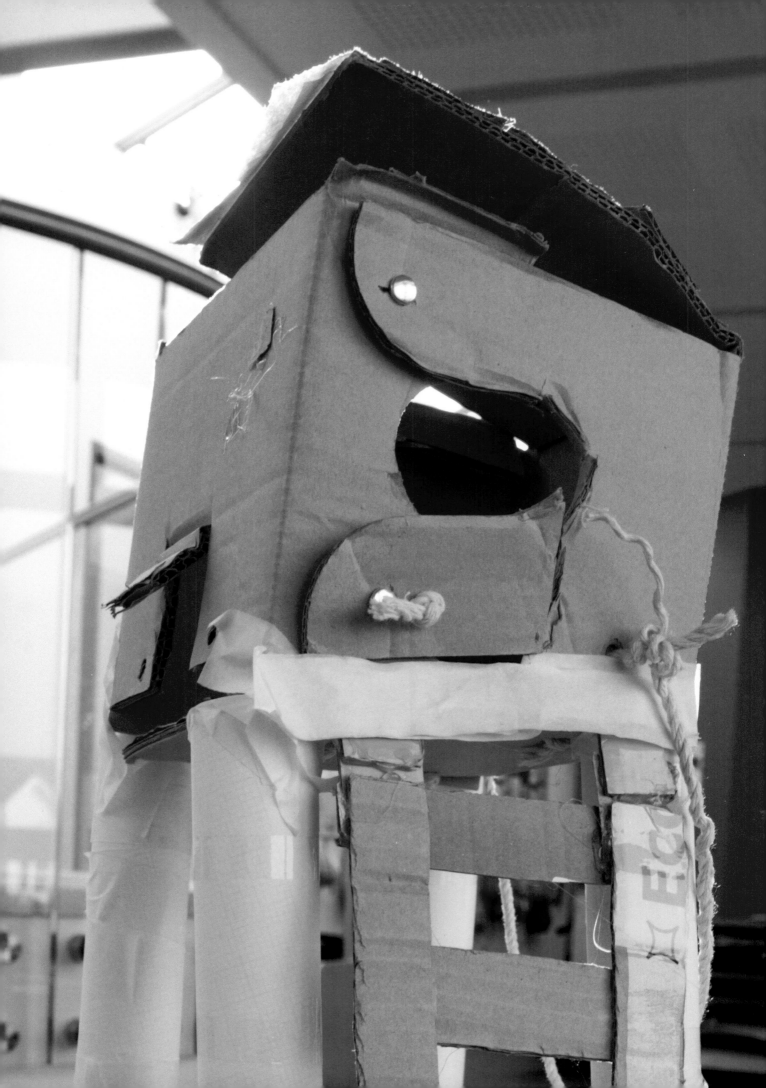

13

Fear and conflict

Session 1

A project for older or more advanced children

This project is more advanced and may be more appropriate for children nine years old and up. They will need to be confident about their art work. They should be used to experimenting and exploring without always looking for end products.

Here are some pointers as to how advanced a class has become: are children happy to explore ideas in different ways? Are children drawing with confidence? Are they happy that making 'mistakes' is part of how to work at their art? Can you list a number of basic processes such as painting, printing, collage and using clay which you know children are confident in using? Is the class used to talking about art? Are they used to talking about their own art? Are children happy to work on a comparatively large scale, say A2 size paper? Are they able to work collaboratively and on their own? If there is a positive answer to most of these questions, then the class is ready to tackle a project of the following kind.

Talking about conflicts

The work could be linked to any situation where people are suffering because of an armed conflict, or perhaps because of a natural disaster such as earthquake or famine. Another possibility is to link the work to projects about the Second World War. Try starting the work by showing video clips of people talking about their experiences, or perhaps some of the miserable conditions affecting their daily life. We found a video clip online which showed children talking about their experiences of civil war in Sierra Leone. Another clip gave a voice to children who had seen troops invade their settlement on the Gaza Strip.

If you lived in a country which had a civil war, or in a town invaded by soldiers, what would life be like? What would be happening around you? How would you be feeling? What would you, your friends and family be doing? What might have happened to them? How would they be feeling?

Introduce the concept of civil war. Do the children know of any other civil wars? Do they know where Sierra Leone is? It might be appropriate to talk about other recent conflicts, for example, in Afghanistan. Perhaps members of their families have experiences as soldiers or as refugees. Children could read extracts from newspaper reports on conflict.

You will need: video clips, newspaper reports; images of war in art and photography.

Above: there are many excellent images of war to talk about with children. This is The Mule Track *by Paul Nash, 1918, © Imperial War Museums (Art. IWM ART 1153)*

Right: ideas sheets provide children with a chance to respond to what they see, hear and talk about

Below: children are able to decide whether to draw, write or both. At this stage, boys often respond with images of weapons, shooting, etc. This first response is important. As the project develops, their responses deepen and broaden

Making written and visual notes about what life is like in a war zone

If you or the children kept a written note of important ideas as they came up during the discussion, this could be used to help structure the visual response.

Now instead of talking about your ideas, I am going to ask you to make some drawings that show what you think is going on if you lived in a war zone, what the people who live there are doing and how they are feeling.

Use the paper and cover the sheet with lots of small drawings. If you can't draw people very well don't worry too much, you could even use stick men if you wanted! It is the ideas that matter. Some of you may want to write your own notes to go along with your drawing. That's fine too.

You could use sketchbooks as an alternative to drawing boards and paper. Later, the children will enjoy talking about their drawings. This is a good time to emphasise how drawings might be used to record ideas, thoughts and feelings in an unstructured and immediate way.

You will need: drawing boards, paper; drawing media.

Session 2

Talking about Picasso's painting, *Guernica*

This painting is widely considered to be a twentieth century masterpiece, showing so clearly the pain, horror and anguish of war. Picasso was responding to the bombing of the town of Guernica in the Spanish Civil War. Unusually for paintings, this work is almost monochromatic, so a reproduction of it could be photocopied and the children could work from the photocopied reproduction in pairs or small groups. Ask the children to identify what they can see in the painting. This project was part of wider curriculum work by this class, so we purchased a poster of Guernica. If you do not have good blackout in the classroom when projecting images, colour and detail can sometimes be very washed out. In this case, you may need to supplement digital images with printed reproductions of the art.

Now use your ideas sheets to collect some of the shapes that Picasso has used. Remember to include the shapes of some of the things you found when you were talking about what you could see in the painting. Remember not to draw everything in too much detail, it is more important to make a good collection of the different shapes that are shown in the painting.

Now discuss the content of the painting in terms that might include what is happening, what is being felt and what is going to happen next. This is a good opportunity to refer to the initial general discussion about what life might be like in the city. Ask the children for their opinions about Guernica. What do they think about Picasso's style?

What do you think about this painting? Would you hang it on your wall at home? What do you like and dislike about it? Why do you think Picasso painted it?

Children may comment how much they dislike the painting when they see it at first, but once they realise how serious it is, they like the fact that Guernica really makes them think.

You will need: drawing boards and paper; drawing media; *Guernica* in reproduction.

Above: these new ideas sheets are a response to talking about Guernica *by Picasso*

Right: the project is extended by looking at photo-journalism

Session 3

Talking about photographs from newspapers and magazines

Here is an opportunity to introduce children to photo-journalism. Photographs carry powerful messages about war. It is not difficult to resource from contemporary newspapers, magazines and the internet although, obviously, this should be done with some sensitivity. Ask the children to discuss the photographs in the same way that they discussed *Guernica*. They can go on to compare the painting with the photographs.

What are the main differences between the painting and the photographs? Which do you think is better, the painting or the photographs? Why?

Black and white photographs can be used to prompt work on tone. Ask the children to make a version of a part of the photograph using charcoal and chalk or graded drawing pencils. A viewfinder may be useful. Talk about the effect that either dark or light tones have; perhaps some of the darker photographs look more frightening?

Role-play and figure drawing

Ask each group to select one photograph.

Decide what is happening in the photograph and what the people are feeling or thinking. Work out a very short scene that will show the other groups your interpretation of the photographic image.

Decide what the most important moment in your scene is. Be ready to freeze like statues at that point.

Think carefully about how your bodies are going to show what you are thinking or feeling. What are you going to do with your arms? Are you going to be sitting, standing, lying, kneeling?

The children perform and then freeze their role-play scene at the most important moment. This provides a marvellous opportunity for figure drawing. The rest of the class can use an awareness of shape and tone to draw simple figures posed in expressive and sometimes dramatic ways. The children will have to work fast as the models will soon tire. This is also a valuable opportunity to use a camera to record the role-play freeze-frames. Are children able to use a camera thoughtfully? For example, have they considered if the photograph will be a detail, close in, or perhaps shot from above or below? How do these various viewpoints change what a photograph shows and the feeling it gives you?

You will need: drawing boards and paper; drawing media including charcoal and chalk; a collection of photographs about conflict; look back at the advice about figure drawing (see pages 62–64).

Top left and right: these are extracts from role-play scenarios, developed after talking about photographs

Right: experimenting with expressing fear. The children will need to feel confident and comfortable about working abstractly and this project is a good opportunity to introduce abstraction and compare these images with representational art

Session 4

Discussing fear

It must already be apparent how much this way of teaching art is married to teaching and learning in literacy. Some teachers have commented that working in this way is justifiable entirely in terms of language development and the powerful motivation it provides for children to talk or write about their own feelings.

The project can be developed further by introducing children to adult writing about war. There are many excellent and graphic reports from journalists who cover conflicts in all parts of the world. There may be an extract from an appropriate work of fiction to read at this point. Obviously, any extract must be sensitively chosen.

The focus is now the emotion or feeling of fear. The class can go on to discuss what it is like to feel afraid. Ask the children to talk about their experiences of fear.

Have you ever been in frightening situations yourselves? Can you describe what happened? How did you feel? What happens to your body when you are afraid? Is it like being happy and content? Why not? What are the main differences?

It is helpful if children begin to identify words and phrases like: 'shaking', 'goose flesh', 'hair standing up', 'rooted to the spot', 'feeling sick', 'confused', 'empty', 'not knowing what is going to happen next', 'lost' and so forth.

You will need: carefully selected adult writing about war.

Experimenting with colours, shapes, lines and marks to express fear

One of you said that when you are afraid, you shake with nerves. What kind of mark could you make on the board that looks shaky or nervous? Can anyone else suggest a way of making a mark that could show how they felt when they were afraid?

What colours are usually associated with fear? What colours or combinations of colours go with your sense of fear? Is red the only kind of colour that can show fear?

Someone else commented that they felt frightened in claustrophobic – closed in – situations, can anyone think of a way that you could show a feeling of claustrophobia by just using shapes, without drawing a picture? How could you make a shape look nervous? How could you make shapes look confused? I would like you to experiment with different ways of showing fear without drawing a picture. You can use shapes, colours, lines and marks and any combination of these. There are different media for you to use, so try out different materials for your idea. It is important not to try and draw a picture, and you can experiment with a number of different ideas.

It is better to use large sheets of paper and drawing boards for this activity. This work is abstract, although in a rather literal way. Remind the children about not drawing pictures. Encourage them to come up with a range of ideas to start with. Let them use a number of different kinds of drawing media.

This activity will work well with paint. It is also easily adaptable to a three-dimensional exploration using the kinds of techniques described at the end of the last chapter.

Now you have finished the experiments, choose the idea that you think works the best. Use one smaller sheet of paper and draw that idea on its own.

Ask the children to talk about their fear drawings and the thoughts that may lie behind them. Ask the class if they can agree which of the drawings expresses fear in the most powerful way.

You will need: drawing boards and paper, a variety of different drawing media.

Session 5

A final drawing or painting about conflict and fear

To recap: if you have followed the structure of the project so far, the children will have talked about conflict; made visual notes about what happens to ordinary people and children in war zones; discussed Picasso's *Guernica* and collected shapes from the painting; made tonal copies of black and white photos; talked about journalistic photographs of conflict; invented role-play scenes; drawn figures from those scenes that express fear; listened to report-writing about conflict and an extract from an appropriate work of fiction. They have gone on to discuss their own view of fear and experimented with ways of drawing fear using abstract rather than representational motifs. There is much to remember, discuss and look at. The children will have their visual ideas and notes, *Guernica*, the photographs and drawings. They may well have been involved in creative or factual writing.

Think about everything you have done during this project. Look back over all the work. Think up an idea for a drawing or painting that shows something powerful about war in general, life dominated by conflict or your own experiences of fear. You can combine together ideas from any part of the project, or just work on making the best of one idea. You may want to work out what you want to do in rough first.

Some children may produce a powerful visual statement very quickly; others will take hours over their work. It is much the best if you can be flexible about the time individual children take to produce a final piece. Some children may well be motivated enough to work at home.

You will need: drawing boards and paper; variety of different media; visual resources from the project, including access to all the ideas sheets and notes children have made.

Top left: children have been encouraged to experiment and develop their visual ideas and are now beginning work on more resolved images

Top right: this girl is showing great confidence and expressive handling of the drawing media

Right: a detail from a completed drawing about fear

Right and opposite: children completed our project by making imaginary oil pastel landscapes inspired by war paintings of Paul Nash (see page 117)

A conclusion to the work on conflict and fear

This kind of work bridges the gap between primary education that ends at eleven years of age and learning children experience as young teenagers. Art is concerned with expressing ideas and feelings. It is useful in opening channels of communication about deeper thoughts – both for the individual child and the community of the primary class. Important human values can be stressed through this process. Children find a voice to express opinions about the darker side of the world as it is presented by the mass media.

Projects such as this are founded in issues, rather than more formal strategies for teaching art. It is these formal strategies that form the foundation for many of the projects described in this book. A fundamental principle behind much of the work is that children will have more creative choice and be empowered to tackle issues and express more complex ideas and feelings, once a formal foundation is in place. When children can work confidently as visual artists, they are able to express a great deal through their work. Their confidence can be built through a scheme of work that highlights the visual qualities and builds basic knowledge of a simple range of skills and processes. Children who have been given a structure to support visual creativity will be empowered to produce meaningful and expressive art.

Equipment

This list includes what you will need to complete the projects in this book. It could also be used to help form a starting point for resourcing art and design in school. However, it cannot claim to be comprehensive, as this will depend on the resources of your individual school. Many items could be used for other projects which could overlap in so many different ways – for example, you might add paint to a clay tile or draw onto sculptures!

Collage

Scissors

Glue containers

Glue spreaders

Damp sponges or rags

Masking tape for dividing gluing areas from clean working areas

Any type of paper that you would like to use in your collage, plain coloured or printed

If you wish to decorate the paper before you use it to collage, you will need pastels, paint or inks

Roll of thin builder's polythene for covering tables (cut this to the exact size of the tables you will be using in class and tape down with masking tape so that the polythene does not slip)

Construction

Hole punch

Paper fasteners

Wire cutters, (adult use only)

Rulers

Set squares

Compasses

Erasers

Scissors

Masking tape

Cardboard

Raffia and string

Sticky tape

Wire

Willow

Copper wire

Thick and thin grey board or straw board

Art straws

Old newspapers and old colour magazines

Wallpaper paste

PVA glue

Glue sticks

Plasticine

Natural materials e.g. reeds, straw, twigs and branches etc.

Clay

Containers for water

Slip (a mixture of clay and water at a consistency of double cream)

Containers for slip (If these have a fitting lid you can easily keep slip for use on another occasion)

Old paint brushes for applying slip

Cutting mat or sheets of wood to cut on

Old shirts or aprons

Clay tools

Wooden boards for clay

Wooden strips to help form clay tiles (see page 97)

A wire cheese cutter is useful for cutting clay from a large slab, (adult use only)

Rolling pins

Clay (use buff-coloured or red earthenware clay. Use grey clay if you are going to glaze or paint the ceramic objects in bright colours.)

Polythene food bags for preparing the clay by dividing it into these bags

Protection for tables: polythene, as for collage. You could also cut sheets of hardboard to the exact size of the tables (or combinations of tables) used in school. This gives a very effective (and instant) cover, which makes clearing up very fast, and they can be used again and again. A local timber supplier may be able to cut these hardboard covers to size.

Damp sponges

Rags to wipe sticky hands

Paper bags

Newspaper

Cardboard

PVA glue for varnishing

Scissors

Masking tape

Computers and digital cameras

Digital cameras for children to use (video cameras and microphones are also important for children to collect, record and present ideas – animation is not covered in this book but a video camera or webcam together with appropriate software will be needed if children are to go on to animate drawings or models)

Access to computers

Child-friendly paint and draw software

Software for manipulating images

Presentation software (such as PowerPoint)

Access to a scanner

Access to a photocopier/printer

Drawing

Drawing boards – these are vital (use thin 3 mm plywood and make two sets, one large enough to hold an A2 sheet of paper and a second set for A3. A local timber supplier may be able to cut these to size. After cutting, the edges should be sanded or taped to prevent splinters. Ideally corners should be rounded and the boards varnished, although this is not essential)

Bulldog clips

Viewfinders (Small sheets of card with various sizes of rectangle cut out of the centre)

Masking tape

Sketchbooks (children could make their own sketchbooks)

Equipment (continued).

A selection of pencils – 4B pencils, HB pencils, H pencils

Charcoal

Chalk

Soft pastels

Oil pastels

Fibre-tipped pens

Coloured marker pens

Coloured pencils

Coloured felt pens

Black wax crayons

Coloured wax crayons

Fixative for charcoal and soft pastels (use inexpensive firm hold hairspray as an alternative)

Drawing paper (e.g. cartridge paper) in a variety of sizes: A1, A2, A3, A4, A5, A6

Cheap paper (e.g. newsprint) in a variety of sizes: A1, A2, A3, A4, A5, A6

Cardboard, both thin and thick

Large rolls of paper around 1.2 metres wide

Buff and off-white sugar paper

Coloured sugar paper

Tissue paper

Tracing paper

Large roll of cheap paper – (e.g. brown wrapping paper)

Fabric design

Iron (for fabric)

Special printer cartridges or paper (that allow children to transfer designs from the computer onto fabric)

Inexpensive white fabric

Coloured fabric off-cuts

Fabric crayons, paints and pens

Natural materials for making sculpture or weavings (reeds, straw, twigs and branches etc.)

Cardboard, raffia and string

Ribbons and wool

Painting

Sponges

Rags

Mixing palettes (flat). Paper plates work well.

Containers or palettes to hold paint

Containers for water

A selection of brushes (thick and thin, try: round head sizes 4 and 10; flat head sizes 6 and 12; a fine-tipped soft brush size 4; and a range of inexpensive decorator's brushes)

Different kinds and sizes of paper and card

Masking tape

Water based school paint (I recommend ready-mix paint which provides a better quality of colour and is easier to use than powder colour) – you will need a collection of colours that allow children to explore the possibilities of colour mixing. Try: bright blue, turquoise, crimson, bright red, yellow ochre, bright yellow, white and black

PVA glue to add to the paint in case you want to make it thicker

Other paint (e.g. water colours; acrylics, oil paint – however, these can be expensive)

Washing up liquid

Printing

Water-based printing inks in different colours

Flat trays for rolling out inks and mixing colours

Rollers

Damp sponges

Rags

Washing up liquid

Fibreboard of different sizes or thick strong cardboard such as straw board

Cardboard

Scissors

PVA glue

Glue spreaders

Brushes

Covers for the tables

Old newspaper or magazines
Paper to print on

Storing children's art

Clear plastic wallets
Inexpensive wallets for each child to hold all but the largest work can be made by stapling a sheet of strong polythene around three edges of a sheet of A2 card.
Printouts of digital work and photographs of 3D work can also be stored in the portfolios.

Displaying artwork

A stapler and staple gun (adult use only)

Examples of art, craft and design

Schools will also need a collection of images of adult art, craft and design that includes historical and contemporary examples, and examples from many different cultures. The Internet is an unlimited source for digitised images which can be printed out or projected. It is important to check that your school has a coherent policy for internet use. It is often forgotten that there is a wealth of design around us all the time. If appropriate, use examples of fashion, fabrics, interior decoration, cars, gardens, architecture, book illustrations, ceramic items, kitchen utensils, light fittings, jewellery, household appliances, motorway bridges, door furniture, chairs, and so on. Discount book shops often have very inexpensive art books and posters.

Printed images of art are sometimes preferable to digitised images collected from the web as projected or printed images can have washed-out colour and detail is hard to see, especially if black out provision is poor. There are a number of ways of collecting print-based images for free. Collaborate with your colleagues to collect old postcards, calendars, photos from magazines, birthday cards and so on (don't forget to include images of design and art from different cultures). Make sure the school is on the mailing list of a number of art galleries – you may receive invitation cards that have images and even posters. Three-dimensional art is often difficult to introduce using reproductions. Use the examples of public art in your area. Churches and other places of worship often contain beautiful art objects. Architecture is often overlooked as a source of original

examples of design. Some schools build a commitment to visit art galleries into their art policy; a local art gallery may have an education officer who will offer advice. It may be possible to visit an artist's studio or workshop. You could invite an artist to visit school and work with children. Is there a parent who is an artist, crafts-worker or designer? Perhaps they could be invited to visit the school?

All the projects included in *Teaching Art 7–11* have been tested in the classroom and are suitable for the age group. However as with all practical activities, care should be taken with the use of all materials and equipment. Using equipment can be dangerous if children are not warned about potential problems and taught to act sensibly and safely in the classroom. It is the teacher's responsibility to ensure this. The National Society for Education in Art and Design in the UK has more information about health and safety when using materials and equipment. Visit www.nsead.org for more information.

The next steps

This book shows teachers how art can work in the primary classroom by describing an approach that aims to produce confident and creative children who have the means to express their ideas and feelings.

Each of these projects shows the value of allowing a child to explore and experiment; the need to build a foundation of basic skills; the vital role that the visual qualities of art play in helping children understand how art works; and the importance of investigating the context for the activity by examining the subject or theme that prompted the work. Most important of all, talking with children about art, about making art, and talking about the context that gives meaning to art, is central to this way of teaching.

However, it is dangerous to use successful art activities blindly as a recipe that can be repeated again and again. The nature of art means that the result of an activity, indeed the activity itself, is different in every case. The specific projects described in this book worked; they have all been 'tested' in the classroom. Teachers will find much that can be incorporated and adapted for their own art projects in their own classrooms. The details of what could be said to children may prompt teachers to make similar points to their own class. However, each time a teacher sets out to help a group of children, they will use different words. Each child, in every single case, will make a response that is unique.

Many children enjoy art when it seems freer, more personal; perhaps because they feel they are being themselves rather than producing prescribed outcomes. This is in contrast to 'how to do it' activity books (recipes that guarantee an end product for the walls by only focusing on that end product). Whilst valuable work is often produced, focusing on the outcome can sometimes restrict opportunities for children to work through art to explore and express their own individual sense of their world. There is also the temptation, when writing advice about teaching a specific subject, to devise a curriculum model which could be used as a template no matter where you teach or who you are teaching. But in terms of visual art, any curriculum model is lifeless, some would say useless, without detailed examples of how this personal and creative subject works in the classroom. So, this book is not intended to be a 'how to do it' activity book with a set of prescribed outcomes, or a plea for any particular curriculum model. The projects in this book are simply examples; but they illustrate a set of principles about how art teaching and learning can work well. I hope teachers inspired by these principles will empower children, who will feel they have creative control within an open, and supportive structure of ideas and methods.

Following the first edition of this book, I worked to deepen and extend my approach to teaching art to seven to eleven year olds. I thought about how art made in art lessons at school might embody meaning. Linked to this is how art might be a way to help children understand how culture develops and that

expressions of culture are meaningful. The question was: if children become more aware of how culture works, might they understand and respect cultural expressions clearly different from their own? Moreover, if you design projects for children which allow them to create meaning in the context of expressing culture, are you not also designing projects which allow children to be creative? The twin themes of culture and creativity, overlain with ideas about how to make art meaningful for children, became the inspiration for my own development as an art teacher. Many of the strategies for teaching art described in this book can be used to help children create manifestations of visual culture. For example, they are learning not only how to use clay but that if they can sculpt in clay, they may be able to make ceremonial objects imbued with significant meaning. If you would like to find out more about these ideas, look out for *Creativity and Culture – Art Projects for Primary Schools*, available from Collins Education.

If you have enjoyed *Teaching Art 7–11* and are wondering where to go next, I recommend designing your own art projects based on a set of principles of your choosing. These could echo those outlined in the introduction, or reflect principles which underpin your own art teaching. I also recommend thinking about what art might mean and how art can help children express ideas and feelings as they explore their own approach to the world.

Index